The growing numbers of congregations serving children and reconnecting with their communities through school partnerships isn't just a trend—it's a major movement. Yet there are few published resources to support these efforts. The Mission-Minded Guide to Church and School Partnerships is a case study in how fruitful and spiritually generative a truly collaborative mission partnership can be. While Jake McGlothin's book makes a compelling case for school partnerships, all mission leaders can learn from his thoughtful and intentional analysis of what it takes to engage a congregation in meaningful action.

—**Ann Michel**, Associate Director, Lewis Center for Church
Leade   Seminary

Jake McGlothin will s   schools not only
bless students, but I   h of volunteers
and the life of the church. Jake knows how to create functional partnerships that benefit everyone, and teaches us not to underestimate what God can do through churches of every size who care about kids in their community. Full of practical ideas for sustainable programs, you will find the starting point you are looking for as well as the next steps you should consider. If you feel a calling to serve children who are vulnerable, this is the book for you.

—**Rev. Tom Berlin**, Floris United Methodist Church,
author of Restored

For those seeking a how-to book, look no further! Jake McGlothin shares insights that will enable you to start your own school partnership without duplicating Floris's. This is a well done book that will benefit congregations of all sizes seeking to do community engagement.

—**F. Douglas Powe, Jr.**, James C. Logan Professor of Evangelism
and Professor of Urban Ministry;
Managing Director for The Institute
for Community Engagement,
Wesley Theological Seminary

In my experience as a teacher, mother, and now serving as Herndon's Mayor I've realized that schools and churches share a common goal: striving to enhance our commitment to and support of the children and families throughout our community. I think we can all agree that there is no greater investment to make than in the lives of our children. Our children's future is everyone's future. And they are all our children. Matching schools in need of support with neighboring faith communities who want to serve builds relationships, creates opportunity for advocacy, and perhaps most importantly fosters mutual compassion and a sense of belonging for everyone involved. Church and school partnerships have played a critical role in the success of Herndon's schools and have enriched the lives of not only the families in need but of the congregations who have served. I highly recommend The Mission-Minded Guide to Church and School Partnerships. When we work together for children—everyone wins. I have experienced first-hand the dramatic impact that partnerships have on schools, churches, and the community as a whole.

—**Lisa C. Merkel**, Mayor, Herndon, VA

The Mission-Minded Guide
to Church and School Partnerships

JAKE McGLOTHIN

THE MISSION-MINDED GUIDE TO CHURCH AND SCHOOL PARTNERSHIPS

Abingdon Press / Nashville

THE MISSION-MINDED GUIDE TO CHURCH AND SCHOOL PARTNERSHIPS

This book is printed on elemental chlorine-free paper.

Library of Congress Cataloging-in-Publication data has been requested.

978-1-5018-4136-1

18 19 20 21 22 23 24 25 26 — 10 9 8 7 6 5 4 3 2
MANUFACTURED IN THE UNITED STATES OF AMERICA

For Robin and Mack

CONTENTS

INTRODUCTION

One afternoon our lead pastor, Tom, came to my office and said he wanted to have lunch with Judy, the principal of our school partner, Hutchison Elementary School. As he and I discussed our relationship with the school, he indicated a sincere interest in digging deeper into the school partnership. He thought that by meeting with Judy we could better understand the unique needs of the community. Because I manage the relationship, Tom wanted to get an update on how she felt the partnership was going. So I set up the meeting.

We met at a local barbeque joint. We were aware, in many ways, of the challenges of leading a Title I school. *Title I* indicates a majority of the school's students live at or below the poverty level. When children face problems and challenges at home and in their communities due to economic, social, and/or cultural issues, learning does not get any easier. Throughout our conversation,

Tom asked more and more questions about the difficulties of Judy's position and the challenges her students and faculty faced educating children. She was frank in her answers.

The partnership between Floris United Methodist Church and Hutchison Elementary School was more than a decade old by the time we had this conversation. Many ministries had come and gone over the years. In so many ways, we had helped positively impact the lives of kids and bridge gaps for students, the staff, and people in the surrounding community. Still, there was clearly an opportunity to do more. As we neared the end of our conversation, Tom asked Judy a simple question: "What keeps you up at night?"

The principal paused for a moment, then said, "The summer."

The county school system, feeling the budget constraints that many institutions have faced in the past six to ten years, had eliminated most funding in schools for summer programs. For children without resources, the summers can cause major educational delays that educators call the *summer slide*. It's the idea that when children leave school for the summer, they will lose some of their learning during that time. When children lack involved parents, often because parents are working multiple jobs, or resources for significant summer activities, the summer slide is even worse. They face significant social and learning setbacks because they miss an enriching summer. Children who live in poverty are sometimes left to fend for themselves or are supervised by an older sibling during the summer months. Books or educational materials may or may not be in the home. Children who rely on school breakfasts and lunches may or may not get adequate nutrition. And kids, if left unattended, tend to cause trouble. I should know—I was one of those unsupervised troublemakers. At Hutchison, two other major considerations needed attention. In a home without native English speakers, children reverted to speaking their native language if they didn't have outlets to maintain their English proficiency. Not using English during the course of the summer impacted reading and writing comprehension, potentially causing delays in learning. Gang interaction was also a real concern, even for children at young ages. The principal made us aware that gang recruitment could sometimes start as early as fifth grade.

As we learned about the difficulties of summer, Tom and I imagined working with the school to create a new, enriching, and exciting summer experience. So the next logical question was this: if money or resources weren't a barrier, what would a program look like?

It wasn't until a few weeks later that we actually received an answer to this question, surprisingly a relatively simple one. The principal wanted us to serve approximately one hundred children going into first, second or third grade with fun reading and math lessons and engaging enrichment classes for four weeks during the summer. The program would offer the kids breakfast and lunch and provide transportation. Judy made it clear that just as important as these components, she wanted the kids to have fun during this program. The program would need to be educationally enriching and exciting for the students. Most of the kids couldn't afford summer camps or take vacations, so having a camp experience would be an excellent opportunity for new experiences and learning. If you think about it, doing fun things in the summer is seen as the norm for kids in our country, but that's just not the case for many children living in poverty.

Pulling together a summer program in a matter of months was no small task, but we felt pretty confident we could make it happen. Tom pitched the idea to the congregation one Sunday and said that the only way we could pull off this project was if teachers volunteered their time. He said I would be waiting in the lobby to sign people up.

That day, roughly ninety people signed up to help. We were thrilled at the response, but with multiple people offering to support this initiative we still had little clue on how to develop a summer learning program from scratch. Luckily, two members of the church, with very different skills and knowledge, said they would lead the program with me. One of them even quit her job to help make the program happen for these kids!

Three months later, the first Camp Hutchison, a four-week summer enrichment camp, commenced with the help of nearly 150 volunteers from the church and the community serving one hundred local elementary school students. Camp Hutchison was a whirlwind, a means of grace, and an effort led by the Holy Spirit. It was also a major step and new chapter in our church's relationship with our local school partner.

To think that this program started with a simple question still astounds me. As I sit in my office while the sixth Camp Hutchison takes place through the work of countless volunteers, it's easy to consider how our church and the school would be different had Tom, Judy, and I not had lunch that day, and had Tom not asked that question.

The partnership our congregation has with this local school is a game changer and an integral part of who we are as a congregation. Camp Hutchison is only one of the many ways that we work together to build better community and educate the children in our community. Our relationship with Hutchison Elementary School is now more than fifteen years old and has taught us many things about what it means to be partners, what it means to be more fully present in the community, and what it means to go about living our missional task of loving God and loving neighbor. This partnership has also helped shape the discipleship and spiritual growth of many of our members.

Over the past few years, more and more churches are indicating an interest in working with schools and moving toward making partnerships happen. Hundreds of churches and faith communities have forged this path for us. It's been a joy for me to see what I hope is the beginning of a movement of churches taking bold steps toward making real and impactful changes in their communities by serving schools and vulnerable children. When churches work with organizations, institutions, and agencies that serve vulnerable groups such as children, the elderly, or immigrants, beautiful, God-honoring things happen. These things can be a glimpse into the kingdom of God.

The purpose of this book is to talk about partnerships between schools and churches in a no-nonsense manner, with simple ways to get started and to move forward. I'll cover why these partnerships make so much sense today and why they align with our Christian identity, but just as important, I will provide you with practical tools, ideas, and encouragement as your congregation makes headway into starting a partnership or improving an existing partnership. This book also will contain important data related to children living in poverty and will give you a glimpse of the different players you see in these partnerships: the students, the teachers and administrators, the volunteers, and the church staff. I hope to paint a picture that allows you to feel confident that building a partnership makes a lot of sense as a means to further your discipleship and community engagement.

My hope is that you'll seek the ways your congregation can serve its community, more specifically, its children through partnerships between schools and your congregation. You are most likely just a short distance away from a school that could use your help. While giving you a macro look at why the church and school as institutions matter a great deal today, I'll share practical wisdom, sustainable programming, and simple steps you can take. Just as important, I'll provide means by which you can engage your congregation through sound theology and communications strategies that will create the greatest possible impact.

But First, a Caveat

Before we get into the meat of this book, I want to tell you a story. One of the questions you may ask yourself at this point is: How is Floris UMC able to provide such a huge ministry as a summer camp?

It is a fair question; however, I want to caution you against thinking that we are able to do the work we do only because of our size. Admittedly, it enables us to do quite a bit, but we also refuse to put artificial limits on what we think we can do. The question I always start with when developing a program is the same one I shared earlier: if money or resources weren't an issue, what would we do?

About three years ago, I was invited to speak at a church a few hours south of where I live in metropolitan Washington, DC. It was in a very small town, and the church itself could seat 150 people on a Sunday. The congregants had a relationship with a local school and were looking for ideas to partner with the school in new and impactful ways. I started by telling them about our partnership and the things we do. After that portion of the presentation, a person raised his hand and said, "How many people do you have in worship?"

At the time, Floris had about twelve hundred people in worship on Sundays. After I answered, I saw a number of people shake their heads as if to say, No wonder they do so much—they're a big church! It was almost as if anything I said afterward would not make a difference because they didn't think it would translate to their context as a smaller church in a small town. Comparing ministries in different sized churches is admittedly difficult.

What they didn't know was that I had spoken with the pastor of the church a few weeks before. In our conversation, he told me that they offered a weekend meal program for the kids at the local school that gave enough food to support roughly two hundred kids a week.

What they didn't know was that we were doing a similar weekend meals program and our capacity at the time allowed us to provide food for 150 kids per week. Needless to say, I brought this to their attention. They learned quickly that they, as a smaller church, were having more of an impact in the area of nutrition than the big church near the big city was having. It made them take the work they did seriously and recognize they were making a difference.

What's the point? This book contains a lot of ideas and ministries and principles and compelling messages. This book also contains a boatload of hope that your church can do great things. Transformational ministries and service are my consistent and fervent prayer requests for you and your community.

Do not, under any circumstances, underestimate your congregation's ability, with God's grace and mercy, to make a real and lasting difference in the lives of children. Your community can be different if you seek to make it so. Thinking that you can't do something because of your size will always keep you from attempting something God may be calling you to do. So go after it!

1
PARTNERSHIPS MATTER TODAY

1

PARTNERSHIPS
MATTER TODAY

In this first chapter, I will explain why churches building partnerships with local schools makes sense today. Congregations across the country are starting to move in this direction, and many have already made the leap and partnered with schools over many years and even decades. Partnerships between churches and schools are a natural progression toward meaningful community engagement and ultimately, a glimpse into the kingdom of God.

Generally, when a church is considering meeting a need or building a partnership with a local organization such as a school or social service agency, everyone involved needs to understand the issues surrounding the need. In this case, information regarding child poverty is startling. I'll share some statistics on national poverty and provide you with some of the statistics that helped us better understand our partnership with our local school, Hutchison Elementary.

From there, we will examine some of the risks that children in poverty face in life and learning. We must come to bear that in a developmental context, a high-quality education can make a huge difference not only in the life of the child but also in the communities in which these children reside. I'll offer some insights on why I believe that the church and the school remain two of the most important institutions in our nation. Finally, I will talk in broad terms about the impacts of a partnership, not just on the school and students but also on the church and its members.

Poverty and Children:
Nationally and Locally

Let's take a look at poverty in our country, and how that ignites needs the church can help meet. Since the Great Recession of 2008, poverty in America has become an increasingly visible and challenging issue on America's conscience. It's a regular topic of political conversation. One does not have to look far to find people in our country who suffer socially and economically and communities that have suffered. Roughly 50 million people in America are living in poverty.[1] While great movements in the United States to eradicate poverty have been put forth in our past, rates of poverty remain high and the gap between the wealthy and the poor is widening. This difference just doesn't seem to be that important anymore, which is disturbing and sad. Many reasons for this exist, such as partisan politics, corporate greed, government corruption, and indifference.

The picture of poverty is grim, as it always has been. As Tavis Smiley and Cornel West opine in *The Rich and the Rest of Us*, "We have gone from an aggressive stance on the eradication of poverty to passive, indifferent, and downright destructive positions where the poor are maligned and rendered invisible."[2] In a time of budget cuts, national debt, fiscal cliffs, and political pandering, we should recognize that the marginalized and the vulnerable in our society are most impacted. Children, the elderly, and the disabled live with the consequences from the political ramblings of Capitol Hill, cable news pundits, and talk radio around the nation. The voice of the poor is rarely heard. No matter your political leanings, a Christian should be one who stands on the side of those who can't help themselves or who struggle to live in our society."

If we are to ever see changes to poverty, the people of God and congregations across the country must make a stand and end indifference to those who are most impacted by the ills of poverty. The church must choose the side of the vulnerable, the marginalized, and the oppressed. Christ chose the vulnerable. Churches aligned with the vulnerable often find the Spirit of God with them in their work to eliminate poverty.

According to the National Poverty Center, children make up 36 percent of the nation's poor.[3] For a nation with the greatest wealth, access to resources, and luxury of any civilization in all of human history, so many children living in such difficult socioeconomic situations is unacceptable. Imagine the rows and rows of food at our grocery stores that some children can't access. Imagine the outlet malls of clothing when the homeless have no shoes. Imagine the veteran with a disability who can't access the mental health resources to get his or her life back after the ills of war.

While economic situations in America vary greatly geographically and culturally, we know that poverty impacts the future of our nation, as "anybody who has paid attention knows that the poorer a child is in America, the more likely he or she is to be malnourished, misdiagnosed, and herded into over-crowded, under-funded, and poorly staffed educational institutions."[4] A lot is revealed by the way a community and culture treat the most vulnerable: the child, the widow, the single parent, the person with disabilities, and the elderly person. From scripture, we recognize that Christ chose to engage and heal people in such situations. The God we worship chose to free the slaves, the Israelites, from bondage in Egypt. Jesus met and healed those on the margins of society. He ate with the sinner and brought hope to the broken and marginalized.

As we look at poverty from a national scale, it's also important to talk about the community in which I live. Fairfax County is one of the wealthiest in the country, benefitting greatly from being a part of the metropolitan Washington, DC, area, the seat of power for our country. Many people in this community are employed by the federal government or by a government contractor. Even in the midst of this great wealth, there are areas of great poverty within Fairfax County.

So let me tell you a little more about Hutchison Elementary, a Title I school in Herndon, Virginia, about three miles from our church. First, Hutchison is one of the more challenging schools in Fairfax County because of the very high free and reduced-price lunch population and a large contingency of students who are learning English as their second language. While Herndon itself can be considered an affluent place, the school and the community surrounding it have high concentrations of poverty. Hutchison students face a number of challenges, as revealed through their demographics from the 2014–2015 school year:

- Seventy-seven percent of students participated in the free and reduced-price lunch program.
- Sixty-six percent had limited English language proficiency.
- There was a 22 percent mobility rate.[5]

In addition to these statistics, many of the town homes in the school's boundaries have multiple families living under one roof. Stories of families renting rooms and even couches in homes with many other families are common. A number of safety issues exist when children are unsupervised in homes with strangers living there. In addition, many of the parents have to work multiple jobs in order to make ends meet and thus aren't available to help their children with schoolwork. Based upon a 2015 report from the National Low Income Housing Coalition, a person making the minimum wage would have to work more than 155 hours per week to afford a two-bedroom apartment in our community.[6] Of course, because many parents don't speak English, the lack of even rudimentary English in the home creates a number of challenges not only for the child's education, but also for the school's ability to partner and communicate with parents.

Even with these disheartening statistics, I also want to be very clear about something: there is much to be excited about at Hutchison Elementary. The school is very proud of its diversity, as the student body represents more than twenty-eight countries. The school also has some of the most dedicated and loving teachers that I have ever encountered. And finally, the school has a number of partnerships, including ours, that work together to serve the students. The school improves its test scores consistently every year as well.[7]

While you may be struggling with and feel overwhelmed by the challenges both in our nation and also within communities with significant poverty, you are surely feeling pity or empathy. But let me be clear: these feelings should also be a call to action. Feeling compassion isn't enough; it must be acted upon. Just look at Jesus and what he did when he had compassion for others he encountered in his earthly ministry!

Risks of Poverty for Children

While I was sitting with a group of church members discussing some strategic planning for the church, we were talking about the work of the church through our partnership with Hutchison Elementary School. Specifically, we were talking about children living in poverty in our community and what type of work we could do to help them. While our partnership with Hutchison is the primary means by which we work with children who are underserved and under-resourced, we also talked about the ways we support social service agencies and homeless shelters, which, sadly, also have to provide services and support for children. As we spoke, one of our members looked at me and said, "You know, it's just hard to learn with an empty stomach."

Even though this statement was uttered years ago, I still remember it vividly because of its deep truth and its simplicity. Hungry kids struggle to learn. This is just one of several risks that children in poverty face in our society. In his book, Teaching with *Poverty in Mind*, author and educator Eric Jensen suggests, "Poverty involves a complex array of risk factors that adversely affect the population in a multitude of ways. The four primary risk factors afflicting families living in poverty are emotional and social challenges, acute and chronic stressors, cognitive lags, and health and safety issues."[8]

While it's important to understand the risks of poverty from a research perspective, let me guide you through our experience with Hutchison and the risk factors associated with poverty in this community. Hopefully, this will encourage you to partner with your congregation to do thinking and discovery around this issue in your community. The major challenges that exist at Hutchison include these:

RISK FACTOR #1: HUNGER

First, many of the kids are food insecure. Anyone who has children knows how much kids eat and their grocery bills can attest to that. Children who are nutrition-insufficient have a harder time learning and growing because they are simply not getting enough calories for their growing bodies and minds. The rumbling of one's stomach can certainly inhibit one's ability to pay attention.

RISK FACTOR #2: ENGLISH AS A SECOND LANGUAGE

Many of the children who attend Hutchison are learning English as their second language. This means that they are already behind on their learning because they are also trying to learn math, science, and the like in a foreign language. The summers are also a challenge for them when they have no means to practice and read English.

RISK FACTOR #3: MULTIFAMILY HOUSEHOLDS

Many of the students are living in multifamily households. I am not talking about duplexes and fourplexes, but rather the cost of living is such that many families have to rent homes together in order to afford them. So, a family of five may have one room in a larger home. The family may or may not know the other families or individuals in the home, which raises concern about safety.

RISK FACTOR #4: LACK OF SUPERVISION

Many low-income parents have to work multiple jobs in order to make ends meet. This creates a number of challenges for the students, as they may not have adequate supervision or someone to help with their homework. Again the issue of safety comes up. While there are some county and nonprofit programs that address the time after school, it certainly does not reach all children who could benefit.

RISK FACTOR #5: HIGH MOBILITY RATE

The mobility rate, or the rate at which families move from area to area, school to school, is significant, causing interruptions in learning as they move from one place to another.

Knowing these things in our context, we can understand why children's education may suffer in some way or another. A child who is hungry or who doesn't have resources or support can experience serious challenges to their education. In many ways, the deck is essentially stacked against low-income children as their home lives often create additional barriers to learning. These children suffer at no fault of their own. Say what you will about poverty and its causes; the truth of the matter is that as a nation, and as the church, we should ask ourselves whether we are okay with children having so many barriers to an excellent education.

Education as a Tool for Development

Considering the importance of education, not only on our individual lives but on our nation and our future, is imperative. Education is a means of development, perhaps the best means in the United States (and other parts of the world for that matter) where public education is a right for all children.

Just as we, as Christians, believe that God offers an abundance of grace and forgiveness to all people through Jesus, we as a nation hold to the idea that all children should be able to access a high-quality education. I believe that as Christ followers, we care enough about our future as a nation to put as many resources as possible in place to ensure vibrant and fruitful futures for all children. Education has a direct impact on children's quality of life and their prospects in the future. If we believe this to be so, then we must create resources for our children, not just through government funding, but also through community organizations that have a vested interest in the future of our nation. And if any institution in our country should care about the character development and wholeness of students, it is the church!

Education is an investment in the future, especially for children who live in poverty or in difficult socioeconomic situations. We can't dismiss children living in poverty as missed potential; rather, we must see them using their God-given gifts.

Churches and Schools as American Institutions

Two of the greatest and most important social institutions in America are the public school and the church. Most communities in America have a school and a church, usually more than one of each. You are surely near one or the other right now. These institutions have shaped a significant amount of our culture, as our right to worship and our right to an education are cornerstones of the American experience. Just looking back on your own history as a student or as a child growing up in a church, think about the growth and learning that took place. Not just in math and history and sciences, but also how much your character grew, your social skills, and your ability to live in community with others. Churches and schools are consistently used as places of socialization, learning, and growth. Lessons are learned, characters are built, and communities are made. Even with the decline of mainstream denominations, the church's potential influence in how communities grow and prosper can't be overlooked.

Thinking about partnerships between schools and churches, we see that it makes sense for these two great institutions to work together to improve communities. From my perspective, the partnerships of schools and churches in communities can be mutually beneficial in so many ways, which I will discuss later in this chapter. While you and I may not believe the same things or have the same vision, we can probably agree that both schools and churches are deeply interested in helping people learn and work toward wholeness and better character.

Because of the many challenges children in poverty face and the church's biblical mandate to serve vulnerable people, churches and schools should make efforts to partner where they are able by sharing human, material, and financial resources. For churches in communities that suffer from major socioeconomic issues, the need for partnership is even greater for children who are under-resourced and lack opportunities for continual growth. The church should also seek to serve vulnerable populations where they have the human and capital resources available and partner with the schools whose mission is to improve the education and ultimately the quality of life of children. Congregations should seek to protect those who cannot protect themselves, in this case, children. Partnering with schools is a Matthew 25 opportunity for congregations. When Jesus says, as he does in Matthew 25, the way you treat "the least of these" is the way you treat Jesus himself, the manner by which you feed the hungry, clothe the naked, heal the broken and sick indicates the care and compassion that you show to Jesus.

By the same token, schools offer churches an opportunity to better understand the community and its challenges. Schools tend to be microcosms of the greater community; by working with local staff, families, and children, congregations can learn more about their communities and seek ways to be more engaged in community development and building. One simple way to learn more about the state and future of a community would be to visit a local school!

Most schools and county governments accept and welcome business and faith community partnerships. For example, Fairfax County has an office dedicated entirely to business and community partnerships. Relationships can begin as simply as your pastor making a phone call to the principal of the school and finding out if the church can help at a school or PTA event. Often the pews of churches are filled with teachers. When Floris made its first call for teachers to volunteer for Camp Hutchison, dozens signed up. Regardless of how the partnership begins, what's most important is that the church shows a willingness to be open and available to the needs of the school.

Whom Are Partnerships For?

While researching and brainstorming for this book, I tried my best to consider all the different scenarios as to why someone would pick it up. See if any of these reasons resonate with you:

- Your church has seen significant decline and has come to the conclusion that it must do a better job engaging its community.
- Your church already has shown vitality in so many ways but wants to find better ways of interacting and serving children who live in poverty.
- You are a layperson who has genuine interest in this topic because you've spent years volunteering at local schools.
- You are a pastor who senses the Holy Spirit moving you toward a nearby school.
- Your church doesn't reflect your community any longer and you want that to change.
- You already have a partnership but want to make it better.

Whether you are in a growing church or one that is losing members, whether you are a pastor or a layperson, young or old, new to Christianity or someone who's lived a life of faith for many years, this book is for you. The reason is simple: partnerships with local schools are a suitable and perfect mission field for you!

Because a school is a microcosm of the greater community, you see the same opportunities and challenges in a school that you see in your community. Parishioners with children have a vested interest in their children's education and, if they are even somewhat committed Christians, they appreciate any movement toward wholeness and better educational resources and opportunities for children. For those in your congregation who work, opportunities can happen on the weekends and evenings. For those who are retired, surely a child would love to read with them, or a librarian would be excited to have a few people helping with shelving books. Big or small projects, old or young church members, you can find something for everyone in partnerships between schools and churches. Just take those first few steps toward building relationships.

The Impact of Churches on Schools

When churches make intentional decisions to reach out to their neighbors in positive and impactful ways, great things can happen. In the case of partnerships between churches and local schools, it's important to remember, as we mentioned earlier, the many challenges we have in our nation that relate to poverty.

Schools with high or even moderate poverty rates will have particular challenges that are unique to that community. Many schools, even schools that don't have high poverty rates, have unique challenges and unique opportunities for partnership that can lead to transformation.

Churches as groups of like-minded people who are interested in making a difference can impact the needs of students, teachers, parents, and the greater community if they choose to do so. Many schools have physical needs, such as snacks or other supplemental food needs for students who are food-insecure. Many schools have supplemental educational needs, such as volunteers who read with kids on a regular basis, or groups providing enriching after-school programs. Many schools also have mental health needs, not just for counselors and social workers, who are vital and fundamental in today's schools, but also students and teachers need cheerleaders in the form of mentors and advocates. Students and teachers today need people who invest time and energy in the learning and celebrating the successes that happen in schools. All of these needs can be met by a local church.

At the end of the day, even small churches have resources they can share with a school. Three in particular come to mind:

1. Churches can provide schools with human resources through the work of trained and passionate *volunteers*. They can act as mentors, after-school volunteers, classroom assistants, and the like. They can provide support, encouragement, and learning to students in a committed fashion.

2. Churches can provide schools with *material resources*. Sometimes this may be food, sometimes it may be donations of clothing or other durable goods. Churches are filled with people driven by their faith to give generously. With this in mind, churches can also provide financial resources to help with special needs and funds for particular programs.

3. Most important, churches can provide schools with the opportunity for *deepening community*. Churches can become advocates for schools. The church is a gathering of people who can have

real and tangible impacts. And there is power in numbers, collective interest in solving problems, and communities that can enable and enlighten a widening circle of people. Churches, by getting involved in schools, can show that communities can have meaningful and mutually beneficial relationships even in the brokenness of today's society. In our world of brokenness and fractured community, these partnerships can be a glimpse into the kingdom of God.

The Impact of Schools on Churches

While it is of utmost importance to understand the impact that churches can have on schools, it's also important to recognize the impacts that schools can have on churches. At the end of the day, successful partnerships should be mutually beneficial, especially when resources are being shared.

1. Schools can help deepen a church's sense of mission in the community. The excitement of mission trips to foreign lands leads to the idea that if you want to be transformed through missions in a church environment, you have to go on a mission trip. While there is much to be said about short-term missions and what they do for spiritual transformation, something powerful happens when a church and its members make a sustained,

long-term commitment to another institution in its community. The number of people I've met whose lives have been changed because they took a leap of faith to serve the children within our partnership grows daily.

2. Schools can give members a better understanding of compassion and justice. Issues of oppression and poverty can be very hard to understand, especially when you only look at data. Realizing that millions of children live in poverty in the US can be very overwhelming and hard to wrap your brain around. We can be desensitized by the sheer breadth of the challenges and issues we face in our communities. Schools are microcosms of the community. While you may not be able to fully understand poverty as a whole, getting to know children who struggle can help members have a better understanding of the issues, thus growing their compassion. With compassion comes a quest for justice on behalf of those who can't advocate for themselves.

3. Schools align churches to their community, and schools give church members purpose. It is one thing to profess one's faith, it is another thing to live it out in the world. Words like "relevant" and "authentic" are thrown around haphazardly by church pundits seeking to make churches more attractive to their communities with very little

consideration on how churches interact with their communities. Churches that take the needs of the community seriously, while sharing a common vision of compassion and mercy, will see the fruits of their labor.

A word about motive: children do not need to be our examples, our test cases, to make us feel better about who we are. It is easy to be quite pessimistic about a church helping a school. The real purpose of these partnerships is creating relationships that are life-changing. A child who has a helping hand and a trusted mentor may have more confidence, and a person who is seeking to serve may grow in other ways because of that relationship. These partnerships must be seen as mutually beneficial because they are relationships, not transactions.

If a church earnestly wants to make a difference in its community, the data and reasoning are clear: partnerships with schools can make a tangible difference in the lives of children and in your congregation. If the vulnerable in our communities can't rely on the church to be an advocate and servant, then it's hard to say the church really matters. Getting past the rhetoric and our fixed notions about poverty, the church has a unique opportunity to bring hope and healing to communities. In my opinion, schools are the right place to make that difference.

2

PARTNERSHIPS ALIGN WITH OUR IDENTITY

2

PARTNERSHIPS ALIGN
WITH OUR IDENTITY

This chapter will outline why relationships with schools speak to our identity as Christians and our work as congregations within communities. First, how did Floris UMC began working with Hutchison Elementary School? Our reasoning will give you a sense as to how this congregation came to the conclusion that seeking a relationship with a school was a worthwhile endeavor. Building meaningful connections with schools and with children in poverty is very much in tune with Christian theology and with our Wesleyan tradition and history as United Methodists. Finally, I will talk about why your church yearns for programs and ministries with schools.

Floris Engages
Hutchison Elementary

The partnership between Floris United Methodist Church and Hutchison Elementary School began through a suggestion from a community developer. Floris spent the end of 1999 cultivating a relationship with the Sierra Leone Annual Conference. At the time, Sierra Leone was reeling from years of civil war. The relationship with the church in Sierra Leone ultimately led to the birth of Helping Children Worldwide, a nonprofit that supports the Child Rescue Centre and Mercy Hospital in Bo, Sierra Leone. This organization impacts thousands of lives annually in West Africa and Floris remains an integral resource for the organization. After seeing what wonderful work the congregation could do as a part of an international collaboration, members of the church also wanted to solidify local community work. While Floris had a number of partnerships and programs, we did not have any strategic or large-scale community partners. Around this time as well was a groundswell of ministries in United Methodist congregations across the country seeking to serve children in poverty. Serving children in poverty was a special campaign encouraged and driven by United Methodist bishops who earnestly wanted to see churches help kids. Floris happened to be a church that responded to this call.

Floris United Methodist Church, it should be mentioned, recently celebrated its 125-year anniversary. While the town of Floris now only exists as a small road sign in Herndon, Virginia, the roots of this church runs deep in the community. One very important aspect of this church is that ingrained in the culture of the church is service. Floris has multiple, decades-old partnerships with social service agencies. Many of these partnerships center on children and families, poverty, and hunger.

Enlisting the help of a community developer, church leaders and members sought to find how they could best serve their community. The community developer suggested a very simple solution: if you want to make a difference, go to Hutchison Elementary School. At the time, it was a high poverty school, as it is today. Soon afterward, the church reached out to the school administrators, and they began working together on projects to help the kids at the school. While the work with the school began in earnest in the late 1990s, an official partnership was developed in the early 2000s.

Many of the programs were started and managed by small groups or Bible study group members who wanted to work on a particular issue. Many of the first programs involved material or human resources, such as donation programs and mentoring. A number of these programs from the beginning are still in existence. Later in the book you will learn about some of the earlier ways our partnership was organized and managed. Through this fifteen-year-old relationship, we've seen a number of iterations, ministries, and programs throughout the partnership. One thing is clear: Floris sees this partnership as integral to who we are as a congregation and what we value as a community of believers. In speaking with a few members who were engaged early in the partnership, I also learned that one of the assistant principals at the time we first contacted the school was married to a United Methodist pastor. I have no doubts this made a difference when we started volunteering and serving the school.

In 2010 and 2011, Floris's relationship with Hutchison took on new life with changes in missions and outreach leadership at the church, the advent of a strategic priority on children in poverty, and a new initiative called Camp Hutchison, a summer enrichment program. This program, you will recall from the introduction, became the flagship of the relationship between the church and the school. With these changes came new opportunities and new challenges in partnership development and congregational engagement. Even today, we continue to learn and grow together in the ways that we work together.

The Christian Identity and Working with Children

As we dig deeper into school partnerships together, it is very important for us to consider the ways that community partnerships with organizations that help or serve vulnerable populations are aligned with our Christian identity. As Rev. Becca Messman, a pastor of a Presbyterian church with a local school partnership, said to me, "Partnering with local schools is a means of living out the gospel." For her, to join publicly with folks in your community and to see the support raised by those who make this a part of their life is an incarnational way of understanding of the gospel.

One does not have to dig too deep into Scripture to see a few verses that can relate directly to partnerships with schools and this type of work:

GOOD NEWS FOR THE POOR

Jesus exclaims in Luke 4:18-19 the words from the prophet Isaiah:

> *The Spirit of the Lord is upon me,*
> *because the Lord has anointed me.*
> *He has sent me to preach good news to the poor,*
> *to proclaim release to the prisoners*
> *and recovery of sight to the blind,*
> *to liberate the oppressed,*
> *and to proclaim the year of the Lord's favor.*

Our Christian calling aligns us with Christ, who saw the hurts of the world, who saw the pain in individuals and in communities, and who sought to heal and comfort them in the name of his Father. Jesus freed people from their hurts. There are undoubtedly many hurting places in the world and insofar as we are able, Christ calls us to those places to bring hope and good news. As you seek to learn more and act upon the needs in your community, you can find those hurting places. This is our missional task in this world. Floris acts upon the belief these places of opportunities can be schools.

GOD'S CALL TO RIGHTEOUSNESS AND GOD'S PREFERENCE FOR THE VULNERABLE

A scripture that I read rather often is Isaiah 58. In it the prophet is holding Israel to account for its unrighteous behavior, though many believed they were being holy and accountable to God's law. This scripture has shaped a lot of my work in the community.

45

Shout loudly; don't hold back;
    raise your voice like a trumpet!
Announce to my people their crime,
    to the house of Jacob their sins.
They seek me day after day,
    desiring knowledge of my ways
    like a nation that acted righteously,
    that didn't abandon their God.
They ask me for righteous judgments,
    wanting to be close to God.
"Why do we fast and you don't see;
    why afflict ourselves and you don't notice?"
Yet on your fast day you do whatever you want,
    and oppress all your workers.
You quarrel and brawl, and then you fast;
    you hit each other violently with your fists.
You shouldn't fast as you are doing today
    if you want to make your voice heard on high.
Is this the kind of fast I choose,
    a day of self-affliction,
    of bending one's head like a reed
    and of lying down in mourning clothing and ashes?
Is this what you call a fast,
    a day acceptable to the LORD?

Isn't this the fast I choose:
    releasing wicked restraints, untying the ropes of a yoke,
    setting free the mistreated,
    and breaking every yoke?

Isn't it sharing your bread with the hungry
 and bringing the homeless poor into your house,
 covering the naked when you see them,
 and not hiding from your own family?
Then your light will break out like the dawn,
 and you will be healed quickly.
Your own righteousness will walk before you,
 and the LORD's *glory will be your rear guard.*
Then you will call, and the LORD *will answer;*
 you will cry for help, and God will say, "I'm here."
If you remove the yoke from among you,
 the finger-pointing, the wicked speech;
 if you open your heart to the hungry,
 and provide abundantly for those who are afflicted,
 your light will shine in the darkness,
 and your gloom will be like the noon.
The LORD *will guide you continually*
 and provide for you, even in parched places.
 He will rescue your bones.
You will be like a watered garden,
 like a spring of water that won't run dry.
They will rebuild ancient ruins on your account;
 the foundations of generations past you will restore.
You will be called Mender of Broken Walls,
 Restorer of Livable Streets.

          (vv. 1-12)

As you can tell, this scripture could not be clearer about how we should be righteous through our love and compassion for others. It's less about belief than it is about living out our faith. It's not an idle compassion, but rather a calling to us to break chains and get our hands dirty in the business of wholeness and reconciliation. As you study the scripture, hundreds of verses point at our collective task of loving our neighbor and seeking compassion and justice in our communities and our world. At the end of the day, churches making efforts to serve their local communities through school partnerships is theologically sound. Just take some time to read the Gospels, especially Luke. As the body of Christ today, we must articulate a theology with justice and compassion as core values. In a world more connected and yet seemingly more broken, Christ's call for love and neighbor have never been louder for those who are followers. And it's in reconciliation with Christ that we find new life. This new life begs for restoration and wholeness for the suffering of the world.

The calling to serve the oppressed and hurt is centered on Jesus Christ, whose character, humanity, and love were on full display and remain in action today through the gospel stories and the body of Christ, as we are able to proclaim the love, justice, and reconciliation of God. In his book *God of the Oppressed*, theologian James Cone gives us a view of a theology concerned with poverty and justice. "Christian theology is language about the liberating character of God's presence in Jesus Christ as he calls people into being for freedom in the world."[9] The entirety of scripture declares God's love for freedom and justice, as proclaimed by the prophets such as Isaiah and Jeremiah and Pauline stories of the sacrificial giving of the Macedonians to the Christians of Jerusalem. Our faith leads us toward love and justice. Our faith should lead us to engaging people who suffer or who need help and healing.

Let us not forget our forebears who have come before us and have sacrificed to make the world better. Tavis Smiley and Cornel West suggest that: "Great social change requires persons who possess the courage to tell the truth, to fight for justice, and to be so committed to that truth that they are willing to risk death. No small matter." [10] While the universal church's history is not all rosy and perfect, one can't deny the amazing advances for social justice and for those living in oppressed or in poverty-stricken situations that have occurred because courageous people of faith made it their mission in life to combat the ills of the world. One only has to look back in history only as far as Mother Teresa and Martin Luther King Jr. to see this.

While the Mother Teresas and Martin Luther Kings of the world come to us only once or less in a generation, millions of Christians, throughout the history of the church, have also acted compassionately and lovingly to a broken world. Countless instances of kindness, service, and generosity have been shown to people in need. No big pronouncements were spoken, no parades were run; good Christian people just served others. Have no doubt of the multitudes of Christians who have felt so strongly that they died for what they believed was right.

Wesleyan Theology and Tradition

Before discussing John Wesley and Methodists, a caveat. I was born, baptized, and raised UMC and I work for a United Methodist church. Of course, the context I come from will speak to this reality and thus, it is right and necessary to connect John Wesley, the founder of Methodism, and the early Methodists to this work of school partnerships. If you are not United Methodist, instances within your denomination's history will no doubt lead you to work with people in need, and more specifically you'll discover ways that your forebears sought the wholeness of children. If you are a Baptist, a Presbyterian, a Lutheran, or something else, please keep reading, but consider researching your denomination's work with the poor. What you learn will only enrich your experience of building and maintaining a partnership.

Just as these partnerships make sense theologically, acts of mercy, justice, and compassion are integral parts of being a United Methodist. In her book *Child Poverty: Love, Justice, and Social Responsibility*, author Pamela Couture offers a glimpse into early Methodism and its work of mercy and compassion. "The Wesleys believed that works of piety and works of mercy were 'means of grace' through which God's love could be known and experienced by humankind." [11] The Wesleys suggested that works of piety and mercy were as essential as prayer and fasting. Recognizing, as we move along together, that our work in the community is a part of the sanctifying work God does in our own lives is important. If we are to keep to this Wesleyan tradition, churches must make efforts to be actively engaged in their communities. As one pastor put it to me, a church that isn't engaged in the community is a church on its way to its deathbed. United Methodists have historically been called to do work in the community and as inheritors of this tradition, we find that our survival depends on our willingness to live out the gospel where we live, work, and worship.

And it's more than just donating canned goods and winter coats. We must work not just for but *with* the poor, the marginalized, and the oppressed. Again, from Pamela Couture: "Methodists were taught to provide these services with an intimate, personal touch."[12] Wesley called us to roll up our sleeves and be involved in the work of the world. "Rather than giving relief at a distance, Wesley taught a love ethic that guided personal relationships with those who were in need."[13] Serving children in poverty and church/school partnerships offers hands-on opportunities for congregations to engage in community affairs. It offers us the opportunity to dig deeper into community.

The foundation of our works of love, mercy, and justice is our love for God and our love of neighbor, which Christ called us to and which Wesley would expound upon regularly in sermons: "The necessary fruit of this love of God is the love of our neighbor, of every soul which God hath made, not excepting our enemies, not excepting those who are now 'despitefully using and persecuting us;' a love whereby we love every man as ourselves—as we love our own souls."[14]

When we started our summer program, I asked a seminary professor, who was also a member of the church, to write devotionals that we could share with our volunteers each morning. It was with glad hearts we were able to use these to help our volunteer team members themselves each morning before the kids arrived. Dr. Shaun Casey, who wrote these devotionals, made it clear that the work we did with the school connected to our Wesleyan heritage. He wrote: "As a result of Wesley's dedication to education, Methodists have always been strong advocates of education. One piece of evidence for this legacy is the fact that literally hundreds of colleges were founded by Methodists in America. What you are doing this week stands in a long and deep tradition of Methodists supporting education."[15]

Every United Methodist church I have ever visited has some sense of mission and outreach at its heart and sincere interest in making a difference in their communities. Whether or not that interest is being directed or cultivated is another thing entirely. Our Methodist heritage speaks to this interest as well. This is not a coincidence. Following Jesus and heeding the words and works of Methodists before us permeates through our institution and traditions. We just have to try our best to live up to it.

The Yearning of the Church

In *Jesus Christ for Today's World*, Jürgen Moltmann wrote, "Where the sick are healed and the lost are found, where people who are despised are accepted and the poor discover their own dignity, where people who have become rigid and fossilized come alive again, and old, tired life becomes young and fruitful once more—there the Kingdom of God begins." [16]

Churches have constantly found many interesting ways to engage their communities in acts of love, mercy, and compassion. The sheer breadth and depth of ministries that serve the poor and the oppressed are amazing. Yet I am dismayed by the lack of energy around what many theologians, scholars, and pastors much smarter than I believe is required for the church to live out its mandate of loving our neighbor.

Any work the church does on behalf of the poor, the vulnerable, the dispossessed is just and good work, even if it's not perfect. But we have to put time and energy in this work if we want it to be effective. Not just that, though—the direction in which the Holy Spirit moves us is toward compassion and empathy for our neighbor. This compassion and empathy shown toward those who are vulnerable are in line with the yearning of the church.

This yearning is present in your congregations even if you don't know it. You have people in the pews who are searching for meaning, searching for understanding, hoping to draw one step closer to living lives with and for Jesus. These folks want to dig deeper and do significant things because their faith compels them to do so. School partnerships with churches make so much sense. Many of the challenges schools face are actionable and solvable, especially when concerned citizens want to be a part of the solution. The school is a place that can almost always use the human and material resources that are available to them via congregations. Children are vulnerable. God loves vulnerable people and implores God's people to preferentially treat them with love, dignity, and respect.

This yearning to do more, to dig deeper, to impact your community, can be found through partnering with local schools. Whether you are meeting physical or educational needs, the relationships and opportunities that will grow will astound you. Questions I like to ask churches I meet with are:

- Where do you think God is calling you?
- What issue is your congregation uniquely interested in pursuing?
- Does that issue matter to God?

The theologian Jürgen Moltmann also tells us, "The church is an evangelizing and a liberating community. If it is not, it is not Christ's church—nor indeed a church at all."[17] The church should be representative of God's kingdom on earth, or at least working toward and embodying God's kingdom. Christ called us to love God and love each other; thus the church exists to bring Christ's message of love, forgiveness, and reconciliation to all of humanity. The church should be a community that worships, prays, and serves. It should be a community that cares for those in the margins, and it must be a voice to those who are oppressed. The church must be an evolving and moving endeavor leading us to the kingdom in whatever form that may be. The church must be the physical manifestation of God's loving presence.

In today's world, with its dynamic shifts and interconnectedness, seeking justice and restoration is kingdom building work. Christ's message today is clear: love God, love your neighbor. The church should be the means for humanity to fulfill Christ's demand of us. If one does not care for love and justice and healing, one does not love Christ. The church must love and serve all and be an institution whose mission is the love and redemption found in the resurrected Christ.

While preparing to work on this book, I talked with Linda, who led our partnership for roughly twelve years as a volunteer. As we talked about the different ministries and the people she worked with over that time, I asked her why she stayed committed and involved for so long. For her, it was simple. She was passionate about education and the church afforded her an opportunity for the school to be a ministry for her. She was in a phase of her life that allowed her the time and energy to put into the school, and she loved working with kids. When I asked her what she would say to a congregation that was considering a partnership with a school, she stopped for a moment to think, then said: "I don't think a church needs to know why they should do this. I want to know why they wouldn't." For her, partnerships were so aligned with the church's mission outside its walls and with what she saw as her faith journey that working with kids, she knew in her heart, was a good and just and loving thing. It made all the difference.

Here is a note that Virginia, one of my current leaders, wrote to me about the impact this work has had on her faith:

> Seeing the people who give their time and their hearts to children and families gives me hope. In a time when there is much sadness in the world, I am reminded that there is truly more goodness than evil. About one hundred and fifty volunteers gave up a portion of their summer to help with Camp Hutchison that first year. This includes high school and college students who could have been earning money through a summer job or spending time with friends. Approximately 40 adults give an hour of their week to mentor during the school year, often requiring them to take time away from their workday. In the school, you can see and hear the joy and goodness. And I believe this to be true in the world as a whole. I try to focus on the good in my life and in the world around me. And I have learned to accept that while I can't change the entire world, I can have an impact in the community around me.

Throughout this chapter, it is evident partnerships with schools align with our Christian theology, our history, and the yearning of our members to make a difference in the world. From the prophets to the Gospels, from the early Methodists to the United Methodists of today, ministries and programs designed to serve schools are an opportunity not to pass up when your congregation is seeking better community engagement.

3

STARTING A PARTNERSHIP

3

STARTING A PARTNERSHIP

Let's see where we are. In previous chapters, we've spent time learning about children living in poverty and the inherent risks, and we've outlined how partnerships make sense to congregations in a theological and missional sense. In this chapter, you will learn some simple steps to get started, how to think about the church's role within a new or burgeoning partnership, and finally, some guiding principles that will help you make better decisions and adjustments as you are getting started or as you go along.

Steps to Get Started

After getting a better understanding of poverty, the risks that children face when they are under-resourced, and school's natural synergies with faith communities, your congregation may want to consider starting a partnership with a local school. Here's how you start:

1. FIND A POTENTIAL SCHOOL

When starting a partnership with a new organization such as a school, look to either the closest one in proximity to the church or to those closest to most of your congregation. Do a simple map search. While the former is preferred, it's also clear that in many congregational situations members may drive a significant distance to church on Sundays. Once the schools are identified as potentially partner-worthy, do some research on them. Look at test scores, free and reduced-price lunch numbers, the percentage of children who speak English as their second language, and if possible, see what type of other partnerships the schools have. In the case for Floris, Hutchison had some of the highest poverty rates nearest to us, which made it a natural place for us to work.

You may also want to network with schoolteachers and administrators who are connected with your congregation. Oftentimes, even in large school districts, school staff are networked within their ranks and know the backgrounds and issues of schools and different staff structures and cultures. This is important because you may find that the schools nearest to you have little or no *visible* poverty or challenges that show up on websites or in test scores. You typically find out about these things through conversations and relationship building.

An example: I was working with a group of clergy trying to determine the challenges present in local schools in our community. I reached out to a principal of a school located in one of the "nicer" parts of a nearby town. From a visual perspective, most of the student body appeared to be from upper-middle to upper-class neighborhoods. On the surface, a preconceived notion that everything at the school was perfect was an easy trap. Anyone would have come to the same conclusion.

The principal was frank about the very little "poverty" in the school. But the school also had one of the largest programs for children with disabilities in the county. As it related to partnerships or potential opportunities, what he wanted for his students, more than anything, were trained mentors to help the students on a weekly basis. After leaving the school, I realized this school was perfect for a congregation to adopt. It had a clear and defined need that our congregation could meet by putting together human resources to change the lives of children.

2. SEEK INFORMATION ON PARTNERSHIPS

Another step your congregation should take is to seek out information from your local school district about community and business partnerships. Many school districts have, at minimum, basic guidelines for partnerships, and in some cases, they may even have staff persons who are charged with building and maintaining partnerships within the district. Fairfax County, for example, has an Office of Community and Business Partnerships as well as very clear guidelines related to faith-based partnerships. As Rev. Tim Warner, a pastor I interviewed for this book, mentioned, many school districts also put their strategic goals and mission on their websites for people to see. He also made it clear that understanding the language educators speak and what they are trying to do in a general sense is imperative for your congregation as you are looking into partnership opportunities. Going into any conversations with school staff with general understanding of their work and their mission in mind will only add to the possibility of building trust between your congregation and the school.

3. GET TO KNOW YOUR COMMUNITY

It is important to note that seeking and implementing partnerships requires risk taking and an entrepreneurial spirit. Oftentimes churches spend an inordinate amount of effort on what happens inside of the church, not on what happens outside the church. One has only to look at the life of Jesus and the apostle Paul to know that when they went into the communities, they got to know the people. They didn't stay in one place. Churches that are successful in community engagement must seek ways to stay involved and knowledgeable about the greater community.

As a means to parallel the process of getting to know your community better, encourage clergy and lay leaders within the church to also consider conducting strategic planning and/ or town hall-style meetings to gauge the interests of the congregation.

A strategic first step is to introduce to the congregation that you and the leaders believe engaging the community is important and vital work and that our Christian calling is to be lived out beyond the church walls. Talk about the findings you've gained through your research and conversations. From there, lead the congregation in conversations about their values and their mission.

4. BUILD RELATIONSHIPS

Beyond geography and having an understanding of the poverty or challenges that exist in a particular community, as well as locating any information on partnerships, start building relationships. If after this research you have a few schools or one school in mind, the search begins for a connection of some sort between the congregation and the school. Cold calls or e-mails to organizations and institutions tend not to be returned. That's not to say you will have that experience, it is just helpful to have a person connect you to the school. Look for administrators or teachers who work there first, then parents and teachers from other schools who worship in your congregation. You are really looking for a way to get your foot in the door.

Once a few connections have been made, you have learned as much as possible about the school, and you understand what the school is trying to accomplish, then reach out to the principal to schedule a conversation. Through this conversation you are not trying to start a partnership that day, but rather you are seeking to build a relationship and to understand the school as a whole. Here are some questions you may want to ask:

- Tell me about your time as the administrator at this school.
- What do you enjoy most leading this school?
- Tell me what makes this school unique. Are there interesting things to know about the student body? The staff? The surrounding community?
- What types of challenges exist for your students and staff?

- I've noticed x, y, or z through my web research. Can you tell me about this?

From there, depending on how the conversation goes, tell the administrator about your church and what the church is trying to accomplish. It may sound something like this:

> Thank you so much for sharing this information about your school. As I mentioned, my church, Floris UMC, has been talking about ways to serve our local community. As we did research and considered what our church is really passionate about, we decided we wanted to find a partnership with a school. We believe we can be a part of building a better community through providing human, material, and financial resources for underserved and under-resourced children. If possible, I'd like for us to continue these conversations over the coming weeks to see if establishing a partnership between your school and my church is possible.
>
> If this is of interest to you and your school, what may be helpful is if we identify a few ways that we may be able to work together in the near future and just try it out. We are glad to follow any and all guidelines you have related to working with faith-based institutions and any child safety policies that you may have. In fact, we've read

the county's guidelines for schools working with faith-based institutions and are willing to train and orient our congregation to these guidelines should we determine that partnering on some projects is mutually beneficial.

From there, you may find that the administrator is very eager to get started, or in some cases, he or she may be a bit hesitant to partner with a faith community. In either case, it is helpful for you to be able to answer the easy and difficult questions that may arise, such as "What about proselytizing? Are you going to try to convert the children?" Fairfax County, for example, has very clear rules and guidelines relating to faith-based partnerships, including a no-proselytizing rule. It is incumbent upon you as the leader to have conversations with your volunteers and members about the school's rules. Let me add one caveat: while it is important to follow the rules, you don't have to hide where you're from or why you volunteer. When Hutchison staff introduces us, we are Floris United Methodist Church. Volunteers are welcome to say that they are from the church and to engage in faith conversations should they be initiated by the child. (This will not be true in all schools, however. Heed the rules, or you may lose the privilege of the partnership.)

Once you have a sense that a partnership or a potential project is imminent, build a coalition of interested members within your congregation. How to engage your congregation in the work of your partnership will be covered in chapter 6.

The Church's Role in a Partnership

The church can play many roles in the community it serves and engages. When people mourn, churches can be places of comfort. When people get married, it's a place of celebration and joy. It is a worshipping place and its people are a worshipping people.

When looking at a partnership with schools, or any partnerships in the community for that matter, having an understanding of the church's role is always helpful and brings about better understanding of the relationship. That understanding also gives your members a sense of the importance that the partnership has within the context of the congregation. With that in mind, my suggestion to clergy and laity when they are seeking to be a great partner is to present the following roles.

THE CHURCH IS A SERVANT

First and foremost, the church must be a servant. Matthew 20:26 tells us, "Whoever wants to be great among you will be your servant." For those who want significance and greatness, Jesus tells us we must be servants. Assuming the role of servant is the correct posture for the church to take as it seeks to partner with organizations in the community and the world.

This is not always easily done. When financial, human, and material resources are on the line, we sometimes find it hard to take on the heart of a servant, but we need to go a bit deeper. When the term *servant* is used, a few important things must be considered. First, being a servant in a partnership context means putting the needs of your partner in front of your own. Our ministries and programs can be transformational, but that has to come out of a need to serve, not a need to pressure our partner to do things we want. Being a servant means that you are sacrificial. Serving partnerships, like that between a school and a church, are not always fifty-fifty. Sometimes churches must sacrifice and give generously to their partners in whatever way most benefits the partners. Finally, being a servant means that the challenges the school faces are your challenges, that you see your partnership as an extension not only of ministry but also of your worshipping community.

When I think of this servant mindset the first example that comes to mind is the support we provide annually to the new teacher orientation at the school. We use the church bus to take the teachers around the community with the help of an administrator, and then we welcome the teachers by providing a delicious lunch. We have been doing this for three years, and it's such a joy for us to get to know the teachers early on and show them a great deal of hospitality and welcome.

THE CHURCH IS A SEEKER

Just as we attend to means of grace to deepen our understanding and knowledge of God, so we, too, should seek ways to deepen our understanding and relationships within the community in which we live. The first step to doing this is to develop meaningful relationships with the staff, students, and community of the school. The leaders and clergy are not the only ones who need the understanding and relationships. You should encourage your volunteers to get to know those with whom they will have contact. It is through relationships that we come to understand communities and schools. You should also seek out information regarding the surrounding community. Get to know the social service agencies that serve that community, and review your research including data from a demographic census. If church members genuinely want to get to know a school and a community better, they must seek to know them better in all the ways possible.

THE CHURCH IS A CHEERLEADER

The idea that a church should be a cheerleader was a new one for me, but it is one I found is of utmost importance. Instead of *cheerleader*, I could have used words like *advocate* or *supporter*, but let me tell you why I didn't do that. A cheerleader is an encourager, one who is positive even in difficult situations and cheers for the team even when it's hard. Cheerleaders also provide celebration when it's appropriate.

For churches, being a cheerleader means that the partnership holds a place of honor for the church, and the congregation tries to publicize the successes of the school and the partnership wherever possible. One of the ways Floris did this in 2016 was very simple. The school accepted our offer of hosting its end-of-school luncheon for the staff. It was easy for us to let them use our space. They had a wonderful area in which to celebrate the educators who make all the difference at school.

It is important to highlight the challenges and the difficulties that the school faces and essential also to highlight the good. Congregants should not view the school, the administrators, the teachers, or the students with pity but rather as partners who deserve empathy when it is needed and encouragement and joy when success occurs. Cheerleaders do not just cheer during the good times; they also share the bad.

Guiding Principles

PARTNERSHIPS ARE SACRED, PROGRAMS ARE NOT: ADAPTABILITY

I spent my first year at Floris getting to know my leaders and participating in the different programs and ministries the church offered the community. I began looking for themes, challenges, and opportunities. From the very beginning, the potential opportunities in our relationship with Hutchison were intriguing. We had many active programs and ministries happening at the school, but I could that see some small adjustments could make the relationship a cornerstone in our community outreach and missions.

In strengthening existing programs and showing a willingness to adapt and change as necessary based on the needs of the school, we were able to build a significant level of trust between our church and the administration. Within a few years, we were able to make large and small shifts in our work that brought about significant exposure for the school at the church while increasing our impact at the school.

You have to be willing to adapt, change, or even let go of ministries and programs that no longer serve the partnership in a meaningful way. That being said, letting go of ministries and programs in a church setting is one of the hardest things to do. That's for another book!

One of the big programs I first worked on with the school was our annual used-clothing sale. Years prior, the school had a sincere interest in helping the students and their families with acquiring good-quality used and especially winter apparel. They asked us to make it into a fund-raiser for the school that would meet needs for families such as groceries and utilities. The basic idea was this: Floris would collect good clothing, bags, and shoes for adults and children over a span of a few weeks, we would bring the clothing to the school, and organize the sale. During teacher workdays when families were required to meet with teachers, we would hold a clothing sale where families could purchase items for twenty-five cents to one dollar. So, coats and shoes were a dollar, most everything else was a quarter.

Each year we did this in partnership with the school, we raised hundreds of dollars and provided the school's families with much-needed clothing for students and families as well as funds for food and utilities. As the years progressed, however, word got out to the community that people could purchase clothing for next to nothing. During the teacher workdays, people from the community would line up at the school hours before the school opened so they could purchase clothing. This made it nearly impossible for the families and children of the school to benefit from this sale. Over the course of a few years, despite many efforts from the school and the church to remedy these challenges, the sale became more trouble for the school than a benefit.

They asked hesitantly that we forgo this ministry. While I had members actively engaged in this program, letting the ministry go made the most sense.

As you do a particular ministry over a series of years, you will find sometimes the ministry no longer meets the goals or purposes that existed originally. Sometimes no one minds, but you *as a leader* always have to be willing to drop programs when they no longer serve the partnership in a meaningful and impactful way. The fact that the principal asked us to discontinue this ministry alone made the decision quite easy. Fortunately we had a good relationship built on mutual trust with the school so the staff felt comfortable asking us to discontinue a ministry. Imagine from their perspective the anxiety that could have been present when they had to tell their valued partner that they didn't want its help in a particular zone anymore. That's the type of relationship that you want to work from, one that allows you to have honest conversations about what's possible, what works, and what you should do moving forward.

In the summer of 2015, the principal of the school retired. This person was a champion of our partnership and a dear friend and colleague. As we were learning about the hiring process and the potential of a new lead administrator at the school, we naturally felt nervous. Would he or she be interested in our partnership? Would he or she have any major disagreements with a church partnership? What type of leadership would the new principal bring to the table?

While questions abounded, here is what I knew: First, our partnership was more than fifteen years old, and the county schools saw it as an official partnership. We had solid programs with huge and important impacts on the lives of the students, teachers, and the greater community. While I could expect changes, a smart administrator would *want* us to mentor their students and teach

English to adults in the community, many of whom were parents of students at the school. I believe that we, over the course of fifteen years, had shown ourselves to be a patient and flexible partner, willing to make shifts to better serve the school.

Despite my nervousness, I was pleasantly surprised at how well we began to work with Ray, the new principal, when he came on board. Not only had he heard about our partnership from me, but also through other channels. He knew that we were a valued partner interested in the well-being of the school and the surrounding community. When I first met with the principal, we put everything on the table. We were willing to make changes, eliminate programs, and create programs based on the vision he now brought to the school. Today, we are making some shifts in our ministry and looking at strengthening others in a collaborative way.

START SMART, START SMALL

When you begin a partnership with a school, you can assume there will be a consistent and pervading sense of urgency to do as many things as possible. After all, new programs and ministries becoming available in congregations create a sense of creativity and energy among the members of the church.

For example, let's say that you just decided to start a new feeding program at a local school. You've worked for months trying to build a team, put the resources together, and build mutual expectations between you and the school. Once you present this opportunity to the congregation, you hope you'll get a good response so you can sustain the feeding program over a predetermined period of time.

What will likely happen as well is that people will come to you with different ideas about the same issue, such as nutrition, and want you to move forward on their ideas as well. Please try your best to start smart: avoid initiating multiple programs at once, or more important, trying to appease your congregation by entertaining changes, new ideas, and programs before the one you've been working on has had an opportunity to proceed and succeed.

What I mean by start smart is this: don't get pulled in too many directions, trying to do too many things and trying to satisfy too many constituencies at once, which will have negative effects. Here's what you should do:

- Talk to the school about its needs.
- Find a task or goal mutually actionable and beneficial.
- Build a great team.
- Invite the congregation to be a part.
- Plan and prepare for the project.
- Do the project.
- Review the project.
- Adjust as needed.
- Try to do it again if it makes sense.

This is the formula we use.

Once when we were recruiting for our mentoring program at the school, someone came up to me and said we should start mentoring at a local high school as well. While I expressed my appreciation for her interest, I politely declined. I encouraged her to go to the local school and volunteer, especially since she was so passionate about it. When you politely decline ideas from your congregation, you must be careful how you do it. When you say no to someone who is emotionally vested in an idea, it can come as quite a blow to hear that your pastor or the staff is not interested as you are. The local church can have an impact in the community with its material, human, and spiritual resources, but it would be a mistake to try to solve all the problems in the community at once. It's just not practical or possible.

When you are starting a partnership, starting small is very important. At Floris, we like to take on big, audacious projects, and sometimes I have to temper the desire to do more. I want a program that is well-organized, well-resourced, and sustainable over time. If "Overdo" is the motto for first the year, expectations will be set going forward. Try to meet the expectations put in front of you, create opportunities to achieve a bit more, but don't go too far. Start small and see how it goes. If you find after the first year that you can do more in a sustainable way, you should.

NEEDS PRECEDE PROGRAMS

When you begin looking at the opportunities with a local school, start by seeking replicable programs that serve these types of partnerships. But don't be fooled: just because something works through one partnership doesn't mean it will work the same way when implemented in another state, county, or school.

One size does not always fit all, but it is undoubtedly important not to duplicate efforts or to develop something on your own when it's been done successfully many times before. Always consider what makes your school, your congregation, and your partnership unique.

Many times in church missions and outreach, a church and/ or its leaders approach a problem or issue in the community with a clear strategy that worked in other communities or in other circumstances. It's very important to understand history and context and consider the means by which you are meeting needs. Instead of engaging in learning, many churches proceed with a cargo-drop ministry. This occurs when a church gives a partner or potential partner solutions to the organization's problems without first seeking to understand the specifics about the organization or deepening their understanding of the issue the organization is facing. When churches do this, the effort is at a disadvantage from the beginning.

When going into a partnership, keep your options open and frankly, keep your heart open to where the Spirit leads. This lesson became abundantly clear to me through our nutrition program at the school. We learned about another organization that managed a very similar program at other local schools. We found out the meals they were providing were very different from what we offered, primarily because the cultures they were serving were different from ours. They also organized their packaging of the meals much differently from the way we did. We were both serving a need, but due to the types of organizations we were, our relationship with the schools, and the preferences of the students, we adjusted the program.

THE SCHOOL PARTNER IS THE PRIORITY

A primary challenge that occurs with any type of partnership between a congregation and another entity is the issue of importance. Due to the resources, time, and energy you provide that school or entity, you may feel entitled to a certain level of importance as a congregation within that particular community. This can be a significant challenge.

To be clear, when it comes to a partnership between a school and a congregation, while you may be important, you are not the priority. You may want teachers or administrators to promptly respond to your e-mails and questions, you may wonder why they haven't made a decision related to a program that may happen in the future, and you may not understand why they haven't taken you up on the offer for lunch or some other thing. Just be cool about it.

Schools are in the business of teaching and educating our children. Plain and simple, your role as a partner is to support that work. That means you may provide resources in a number of ways, and rest assured the school is appreciative of your help. But think of it this way: your relationship should be a means by which the school serves students better. Their mission is not to make their partner feel happy and important, though most of them want that, too.

An example: When I first started working at Floris, I asked the congregation to funnel all ideas and opportunities for the school through me, as I wanted to have an understanding the types of requests and interests our congregation had. Also it allowed me an opportunity to filter those requests and opportunities as well, based on my conversations with the administration on its interests.

I was amazed by the sheer number of requests, outside of our normal programs and ministries that were being sent to the principal. Eagle Scout projects, fund-raising ideas, suggestions for new ministries and programs: all of these ideas were going to the principal on a regular basis. And we were one of multiple partners that may or may not have been doing the same thing. When people's roles as teachers and administrators gets clouded by outside opportunities, it can lead to a few different challenges. The teachers or administrators, inundated with requests, may not be able to respond in a timely manner. This always creates interesting conversations from congregation members who may be upset or frustrated that they haven't heard anything. It can also lead to taking valuable time away from teachers and administrators, who again are responsible not to us, but to the children they serve and the community. *They* are the priority.

PUTTING THE PRINCIPLES TO WORK: THE CASE OF FOREST EDGE

In 2014, Floris embarked on a campaign called Imagine, setting out to implement five initiatives over the course of three years. One of these initiatives was starting our first new campus, called Restoration Church.

Led by Rev. Tim Ward, the hope for Restoration was to start the first United Methodist congregation in the town of Reston, which is adjacent to Herndon, where Floris is located. Tim was very excited to get started and build this new faith community. With about eighty Floris members acting as missionaries, he opened Restoration Church the first week of January in 2015.

Tim faced a huge challenge in starting this new faith community: finding adequate meeting space that would not cost too much money. So he started looking at having the church worship at a local school. Restoration was, and still is today, held in the gymnasium of Forest Edge Elementary School.

When Tim was looking at potential schools to host Restoration Church, I was excited when he invited me to go with him to meet with the principal at Forest Edge. This was preceded by quite a bit of work on Tim's part: reaching out to the county, reaching out to the school, and seeking to identify the best place for this new worshipping community. We met with the administration probably two to three months before the first worship service.

Beyond the small talk, Tim really amazed me with how he approached this administrator. While I don't remember what he said verbatim, the gist of it was this: *Restoration is going to be a new church in Reston, and we are so very excited to worship here at Forest Edge on Sundays. While we are really appreciative that we are able to use the space, it is my belief that this congregation doesn't just want to use the space on Sundays. We want to be a part of your community. Are there ways that we can work together or ways that our congregation can serve the school?*

This offer from Tim was without pretext or expectations. In my view it was simply a way for him to say that we wanted to serve. As we got to know the school better, we learned so much about the school, the staff, the children, and the families. This meeting occurred in November, when the weather was getting colder as we headed into winter. The principal responded that the school needed a way to help a few families with purchasing coats and winter boots for some of the students. Obviously the school didn't have a big resource for needs like that. Tim immediately asked if we could provide them with a cash donation from our Pastor's Discretionary Fund to help with any needs that arose. They happily said yes. A week or so later, they received a check for one thousand dollars.

This meeting with the administration and Tim was a great example of how a partnership can start. Tim showed a sincere and deep interest in wanting to partner with and serve schools. He listened to the needs, and he made an actionable response. This meeting set off a great tone that would benefit the school and the congregation in the months and years to come.

So let's think about the principles Tim used in first meeting with the school. First, Tim started small. He wasn't looking to start a giant program or make big waves early on. The school identified a pressing need, and the church responded. He also considered the needs of the community prior to programs that we could offer. For example, he could've brought up the possibility of a clothing drive, which we had a history of doing at Hutchison Elementary. A clothing drive may have taken months to organize, while the need was immediate. Finally, Tim made the school the priority in these conversations. Conversations about logistics and using the building would have been reasonable talking points, but building relationships is more important.

For Restoration Church and Forest Edge, the story of their partnership is still being written. Restoration has partnered with parents, with staff, and with the community to do a number of really great programs. There will be stories to tell in the future on how a worshipping community meeting at a school can engage that school in mutually beneficial work. What is evident today is the love that the church has for the school and the appreciation the school has for the church. This partnership is becoming a sacred part of the Restoration story.

4

PROGRAMS AND MINISTRIES FOR THE PARTNERSHIP

4

PROGRAMS AND MINISTRIES FOR THE PARTNERSHIP

One of the beauties of church and school partnerships is the sheer breadth of opportunities for your congregation to make tangible and lasting impacts on children and their families. In this chapter I'll present multiple ideas for ministries and programs you can use in your church's partnership with a local school. This chapter is not meant as an exhaustive list but rather Floris's experiences over the length of a long partnership. Additionally,

I will describe how you go about determining and then meeting the needs of the school while identifying your congregation's strengths.

Through the course of this book, the following things are clear: schools are worthy of our service and, if we choose to build these types of partnerships, we have to work toward building good relationships with school staff. At the same time, we should understand why this partnership aligns with our Christian identity. With that in mind, let's look at the different types of needs you may encounter in a school environment. We touched on these items briefly in previous chapters, but let's dig a bit deeper now.

Types of School Needs

BASIC NEEDS

A basic need can be anything important to the health and safety of the students: think food, water, clothing, and shelter. You may run into situations where you learn that some or many of the students of the school are food-insecure. Another example may be shoes and clothing. Churches often provide support to the school in the form of clothing, usually winter coats and boots, and sometimes more personal items like underwear. You may also find that the school has very particular needs for hygiene items, such as soap, toothpaste, and deodorant. Either way, churches should be prepared to help schools with these types of needs, especially at the beginning of your partnership. Meeting basic needs is one of the simplest, most straightforward ways for a congregation to respond quickly to a partner.

MATERIAL NEEDS

For low-income families, providing children with backpacks and school supplies can be difficult. Today, many schools and social service agencies work together to gather supplies for students. Partner churches helping with these types of items makes sense. Collaboration with other agencies and groups should always be considered when meeting needs in the community. Churches can and should partner with others when applicable.

SCHOOL NEEDS

Sadly, school facilities and infrastructure are neglected in many communities. To take it a step further, some schools have serious issues with vandalism, litter, and graffiti. Churches should consider partnering, even using Boy Scout and Girl Scout troops, to do beautification. In addition, schools oftentimes benefit from material support relating to the building, like helping to set up a computer or science and technology lab.

FINANCIAL NEEDS

Finally, many schools host fundraisers that support school programs throughout the year. Dinners, food sales, T-shirt sales, and the like are all possible events. What an easy place for churches to get involved! As you build a partnership, your congregation may come up with innovative and creative ways to financially support the school.

Identifying the Church's Strengths

There is nothing quite like a well-defined community need to motivate a group of concerned people, such as a congregation, to get involved in solving a problem in the community. No matter the size of the congregation, when entering into a new partnership or seeking to alleviate a need, you will always be amazed at how the church responds when you share the opportunity in a clear and compelling way. In a later chapter, I'll share strategies of engaging congregations, but in the meantime, considering the strengths and interests of a congregation is important when seeking to begin ministries and programs with local schools.

In late 2011, I asked a group of highly engaged members to work with me to develop a strategy for future mission work. Floris already had a great partnership with Hutchison, but we also had a significant number of ministries with other social service agencies in our immediate community and in the metropolitan area. What we were looking for were themes and potential means of deciding when and how we would introduce new programming.

Prior to this meeting, staff gathered information about all of our outreach and missions work in both local and international settings. The report included information such as the annual cost to the church, how many volunteers served in the ministry, and how many people the volunteers served over a period of time. As we spoke about the different ministries and brainstormed ideas, one of our members chimed in, saying, "It looks like most of the stuff we do is about children living in poverty."

While we did have some programs that served other people, most of our ministries, local and international, had something to do with improving the lives of children and their families living in poverty. The aha moment for us was recognizing that even though we had a diverse array of passions within our church on social issues, we spent much of our energy on kids. What this meant, at the end of the day, was that any and all programming we would consider in the future regarding children in poverty would most likely, given the programmatic details, be well received by the congregation.

The reason this is important is simple: while churches may have multiple areas of interest, such as poverty, prison ministries, alleviation of racism, homelessness, and other worthy endeavors, knowing where your congregation's interests lie, as well as where people are willing to put their time, resources, passion, and energy, is important. The beautiful thing about a church serving children is that the work tends to be a uniting factor among members. As our pastor likes to say, "You can't argue against helping children in poverty."

You may consider reviewing what ministries you do that benefit the community. You may find themes that will help you move toward a better future in ministry in your community.

Replicable Programs for Children in Poverty

In this section I'll provide information about programs and ministries that are integral to Hutchison and its relationship with Floris. I'll include more basic information about the partnership along with four programs and ministries that churches or faith communities can use in their creation of a church-school partnership, as well as smaller projects and ideas.

Hutchison Elementary School was founded in 1975 and has a rich multicultural student population. As I've mentioned, students at Hutchison face many difficult situations stemming from poverty such as access to health care and other social services, lack of proper nutrition, and lack of proper supervision at home.

Floris works collaboratively with Hutchison on a number of large-scale programs. This includes programs such as the Hutchison Purposefully Active in Loving Service (PALS) program, a weekly mentoring and tutoring program; Help Hungry Kids, a weekend meal program that serves nearly one hundred fifty students each week; Camp Hutchison, a four-week summer enrichment program for up to one hundred students; and evening English as a Second Language (ESL) classes for parents and the surrounding community. In addition, other programs Floris does or has done with our school partner will give you a sense of other possibilities that you might consider with your school partner.

1. MENTORING PROGRAMS

One way churches can partner with local schools is through weekly mentoring programs that match church members with students who would benefit from consistent and positive adult relationships. At Floris, we initiated the PALS Program in 2011 after many years of having a Reading Buddies program (more on that later in the chapter). The purpose of the PALS program is for students to have meaningful, caring, and positive relationships with adults.

When the PALS program started, our congregation had the benefit of a very giving and thoughtful leader, Virginia, who took it upon herself to create a mentoring manual. The manual included information such as child safety requirements, ideas of what to do with the students, logistical information about the program, and even research about the impacts of mentoring.

Mentoring children throughout the school year has become an important ministry of the congregation, especially for those members who have flexible schedules that allow them to be at the school for one to two hours per week. As mentors, volunteers act as cheerleaders for their students. Currently, Floris has forty volunteers working weekly at Hutchison Elementary School. Oftentimes our mentors work with teachers to help students master specific skills such as reading, math, or social interaction. While we expect volunteers to commit to one academic year with their students, a majority of our volunteers make multiyear commitments to be advocates for their students. The relationship becomes a fixture in the lives of the students and mentors.

Mentoring is a ministry that requires a significant weekly commitment from your members. Not only that, the need for child safety requirements and adequate training are integral to a successful program. In a later chapter, I'll present ideas for how to manage and implement trainings and orientations.

2. WEEKEND MEAL PROGRAMS

First and foremost, the church should be engaged in providing for the basic needs of the people in their community and around the world as they are able. If this is not abundantly clear, I would encourage you to pick up your Bible and read it a bit! As, "Is it possible to supply all the poor in our society with the necessaries of life? It was possible once to do this, in a larger society than this. In the first church at Jerusalem 'there was not any among them that lacked, but distribution was made to everyone according as he had need.' "[18]

Churches can use some simple strategies, partnerships, and programs to make significant impacts on the basic needs of people in their community. Churches could partner with, for example, Habitat for Humanity, Rebuilding Together, local food banks, social service agencies, and schools to meet the daily needs of low-income and vulnerable people.

For partnerships with schools, we must recognize the importance of proper nutrition in the growth and development of children. In the book *Poor Economics*, Abhijit Banerjee and Esther Duflo suggest, "A child who gets the proper nutrients in utero or during early childhood will earn more money every year of his or her life: this adds up to large benefits over a lifetime."[19] We must also recognize the issue of hunger in today's schools and how churches can respond. "Nearly 40 million children depend on the nation's School Lunch Program for a healthy meal and sustenance at school."[20] School lunch programs for students are extremely helpful—but students are unable to access this food during weekends.

Providing weekend meal programs for children became a necessity at Hutchison. More than eight years ago, Hutchison administrators approached Floris with a hunger issue: counselors and staff at the school were concerned that many children at the school were not getting enough to eat on the weekends.

Floris, looking at other models of assistance, started the Help Hungry Kids program. The school counselors and staff chose which students, through referrals and conversations with parents, would benefit most from the assistance. Every Friday, each child was given a backpack with ten kid-friendly, nutritious food items to take home. In the first year, Floris was supporting roughly fifty children. In 2011, Floris was supporting 125 children at Hutchison and twenty children at McNair Elementary School, another school in close proximity to the church. In 2015, we served 135 and fifty-five, respectively. Using backpack meals, a model that's used all over the country, multiple organizations and churches have also started weekend meal programs with great success.

The number of benefits to this program is great. First, the food is simple and well-liked by children. The food is easy to open and easy to assemble for children. In other words, if it requires a stove or a can opener, we don't allow it. The most any of the items requires is water and a microwave. Also, because they receive ten items, children can share the food with their siblings and others who live in their households.

In many of these programs, the food is provided to the children in a discreet way, as to protect the privacy and need of the students. At Hutchison for example, there is a special bell that alerts children receiving food to come to an office where meals are put directly into the students' backpacks.

As for sustainability, the program can be organized any number of ways. Floris collects weekend meal bags from individual donors on a monthly basis. Using our communications and e-mail reminders, we have developed a cadre of families that make these weekend meal bags their ministry and deliver them to the church. The church has little to no cost except when we decide to do large-scale packaging events, now becoming the norm as the need grows. About once a quarter, we'll invite the congregation to package more than one thousand meals together in the fellowship hall, usually before our evening worship service on Sunday. Other weekend meal programs do monthly food collections at grocery stores and use corporate sponsors as well as other programs that obtain grants for material costs and package the food on a monthly basis. In other words, a weekend meal program can be organized in many ways, one of the reasons it is such a great example. Weekend meal programs meet the nutritional needs of growing children and engage your congregation in serving children in poverty.

While the movement to help children through weekend meal programs becomes more and more prevalent in our communities, one conversation becoming common in these ministries and programs is the quality of the food provided to the children. Most of the nonperishable items are filled with preservatives and sodium. With the obesity epidemic in America still raging, many groups will begin to seriously consider the food that they are providing to children. It is my hope that as more churches take on the issue of hunger in schools, more opportunities to provide children and families with healthier options will be present.

3. CAMP HUTCHISON

I mentioned earlier that our senior pastor once asked the principal of Hutchison Elementary School, "What keeps you up at night?" The principal responded, "The summer." She didn't know what her students were doing to fill their time, but she knew they were losing much of their learning.

Due to economic issues, Fairfax County Public Schools no longer held summer school programs except for special education students. We realized that many lower-income students across the county would benefit greatly from additional learning and enrichment in the summer.

In 2011, reading comprehension was one of the driving factors for developing a summer enrichment program. For lower-income students without access to education materials, parental supervision, or regular English language conversation during the summer, challenges in the fall were huge. According to bestselling author Malcolm Gladwell, "When it comes to reading skills, poor kids learn nothing when school is not in session."[21] Studies have shown, most notably by the Annie E. Casey Foundation in its report called "Early Warning! Why Reading by the End of Third Grade Matters," students who read at a third-grade level by the third grade enjoy radically improved learning.[22]

In Gladwell's book *Outliers*, the author spends an entire chapter on the gap in education between middle- and upper-class students and lower-class students. He suggests that while innovations in class style, reduction in class sizes, and the introduction of new technology may be beneficial for reducing that gap, it may be simpler. In fact, studies have shown increasing the length of the school year for low-income students virtually eliminates the gap.[23]

As I mentioned previously, summer enrichment for children who do not have the means to participate in activities in the community was a major concern for the school principal. For students whose families live at or below the poverty line, summer can be a time of little supervision and educational enrichment. For those students on the free or reduced-price lunch program, a nutrition gap undoubtedly exists in the summer due to the additional costs of food for families. Without enrichment activities during the summer, students may also have difficulty during the first few months of school. Instead of beginning new material, they must spend a significant amount of time reviewing the previous year's curriculum.[24]

As you've seen, Camp Hutchison was planned as a four-week enrichment program for up to one hundred students entering first, second, and third grades, with preference given to students selected by the school staff. The camp was held at the school, which was easily accessible and familiar to neighborhood children. The students' learning focused on reading and math, but they also had an opportunity to participate in enrichment activities such as arts and crafts, music, science, and drama. County buses provided the transportation for a majority of the students, and breakfast and lunch were provided daily through the USDA's Free Summer Meals Program, a program available nationwide. Volunteers acted as instructors and assistant instructors, counselors and junior counselors, nutrition volunteers, and enrichment volunteers. Over 150 members of the church and the surrounding community volunteered during the 2011 camp and 120 in 2012.[25] We just finished the sixth year of Camp Hutchison in 2016.

The benefits of summer enrichment programs for low-income students are many. Students benefit in learning skills and gain confidence; safety, as students are not at risk for unfavorable activity associated with the lack of supervision or boredom; language, as students have the opportunity to engage in an English-speaking environment in camp for four weeks, thus maintaining or strengthening their language skills; and nutrition, as students at risk for poor nutrition receive two healthy meals plus a snack each day.[26]

Based on assessments performed by Hutchison staff and Camp Hutchison volunteers during the first year of camp, math scores improved for a majority of the students. In fact, students posted an average increase of 20 percent or more over the course of the camp. Reading assessments were based on Developmental Reading Assessment (DRA) scores. The DRA is performed at the beginning and end of each school year. When this past year's DRA scores were compared against the DRA scores from the fall for the students who participated in Camp Hutchison, 92 percent either maintained or improved their reading scores over the summer.[27]

Volunteers also reap many benefits from this camp due to the personal involvement and satisfaction gained from working one-on-one with children who are eager to learn. Despite the long hours and unanticipated challenges, all volunteers remained committed and enthusiastic, even those who worked all four weeks of camp.[28] I think about one of my first leaders for the camp—Susie.

Susie is a longtime member of the church. She first started going to Floris when she was volunteering for a free clinic in another part of town. Susie volunteered to serve the school in several ways, such as participating in Read Across America and packaging meals for the kids on the weekend. In 2011, Susie helped plan and implement the first Camp Hutchison. She had a unique experience participating in the first camp. When we first started recruiting, Susie was experiencing significant job dissatisfaction. She had gotten to a point where she felt she needed to do something that mattered beyond getting a paycheck. She wanted to spend her time helping people. The recruitment for camp really pushed her over the edge. She decided to take a six-month leave from her paid employment to figure things out.

Susie said, "The work at Hutchison made me realize that I had to take a leap of faith and trust God in those things [I am] called to do. It takes so little to do so much for a child. Your time is such a gift and has such a huge impact on the kids." Our work at Hutchison gave Susie an opportunity to focus on something greater than a paycheck. Making this leap was hard; it was exciting; it was exhilarating. Her experience helped her realize how she could live out her faith. She is now in seminary discerning a call to ministry.

4. ENGLISH AS A SECOND LANGUAGE

In addition to the three programs and ministries I mentioned above, which apply specifically to children in poverty and school partnerships, one more program I believe is applicable. Offering English as a Second Language (ESL) classes is a game changer for adult learners. If a church is working with a school with a large immigrant population, a need for English language learning skills for adults is highly likely.

Two primary reasons for a congregation to get involved in adult English language learning are compelling. First, a parent who is able to communicate with a teacher or help children with their homework is a parent who is more likely to be engaged in a child's education. Second, an adult's ability to communicate in English has a direct impact on his or her ability to interact in American society; including the workplace, social service agencies, law enforcement, and doctors. Churches and schools can partner to create evening ESL classes at schools, which are known entities to parents and the surrounding community. For congregations, ESL courses create opportunities for cross-cultural understanding. Many of your members live in a bubble. People in general do not put themselves in the position to know or understand the situations or lives of immigrants in America or of people who are different from themselves. In the teacher/student relationship, cross-cultural understanding occurs and often volunteers and participants begin to seek out additional ways to engage immigrant communities to improve their livelihoods and communities.

The logistics of the program are quite simple. English language classes, both basic and advanced, are provided twice a week, Tuesdays and Thursdays, from 7:30 to 9 p.m. from September to April. Teaching teams are comprised of lead instructors and assistants. We have well over forty volunteers, many having made a multiyear commitment to the ministry. We typically start with about 150 to 200 students and hold parties and celebrations throughout the year. Some important changes have happened in this ministry over the years, which I will outline in the next chapter.

Additional Ideas

In this section, I will share a few other programs we have either used at some point in the past or we have considered doing in the future. These are ideas to consider as you seek to develop your partnership and create ministries that have a positive impact on students and staff.

CHRISTMAS GIVING

For a number of years, Floris has done what we call Advent Giving, which seeks to bless the community with gifts from the congregation. Each year, we assist organizations such as homeless shelters, children who have incarcerated parents, a domestic violence shelter, and organizations that serve children with disabilities with gifts for the children and/or supplies and materials the organization desperately needs. We also include Hutchison in our annual Advent Giving.

To give you an understanding on how this program works, volunteers seek out gift lists from organizations, usually in the twenty-five- to fifty-dollar range. From there, we make ornaments that represent individual needs of families or organizations and put them on Christmas trees within the fellowship hall. On specific Sundays, the congregation can choose and register the ornaments they would like to purchase for that organization. They bring the gifts back to the church a few weeks later. In the past five years, we've received anywhere from 1,200 to 1,700 gifts to give to the community. The Advent Giving program inspires generosity. Families love it because they can teach their children about giving to others in the Christmas season.

While we have typically served individual families by working directly with the school social workers and counselors, the past few years have shifted for us based on conversations with the staff. Because the need is so great at the school, the counselors believed it was becoming increasingly difficult to identify the families who would benefit the most because the need was so very high. Therefore, we sought to do a few different things over the years. We've created ornaments for heavy winter coats, hats, and socks the school could use for children who lack adequate clothing, and we've collected books, games, and grocery gift cards for families who participated in our Help Hungry Kids program.

The Advent Giving Program is also a meaningful opportunity for your congregation to get a better understanding of the needs in the community. In the time of Advent, when we are waiting upon the birth of Christ, it's amazing to see the generosity that people will show once they understand the needs that community organizations have.

READING PROGRAMS

Reading programs require very few financial and material resources. Before we started mentoring students, we had a Reading Buddies program. The children and adults came together to focus on reading books together. Whether held during lunch or after school, reading programs are an excellent opportunity many schools may already have in place so you can just connect your congregation to them. I'll also add that each year, many if not most elementary schools celebrate Read Across America, which is held on Dr. Seuss's birthday. Typically schools invite partners, businesses, and parents to visit the school and read their favorite books to classes. It's a small but impactful program a congregation could easily get involved in.

STAFF APPRECIATION

A simple thing for your congregation to consider is working on ways to show appreciation and give support to the school staff. As mentioned earlier, your pews are filled with teachers, retired teachers, and other educators, and they would probably tell you how difficult their work is on a day-to-day basis. Educating our children is a noble but underappreciated vocation. Just ask if you want to know ways you can show support. As an example, a small group Bible study has offered an appreciation potluck lunch since the beginning of the partnership. This group brings delicious food to the school and the teachers look forward to it every year. A church could offer the potluck for all the teachers or for just one grade.

BEAUTIFICATION PROJECTS

Many churches today have volunteers who are interested in getting their hands dirty. Boy Scouts need to work on their Eagle Scout projects, teens need to do service hours, and retired folks love to garden and paint and do other types of handyman-type activities. Opportunities always exist at your local school to work on beautification and general upkeep projects. When the community comes together to improve the look and feel of the school, parents, teachers, and students notice. A great sense of pride can develop as well. A Boy Scout can build a garden with a science club or find an opportunity to partner with the PTA to paint the hallways and classrooms or do landscaping. Many schools are in disrepair and would probably welcome any and all assistance to make the school look better.

A Friendly Reminder:
These are Replicable Programs

The programs I've mentioned are ultimately successful because they meet the needs of the students, the parents, the staff of the school, and the greater community. They can be resourced through a church's human and/or capital resources. Most important, they offer the congregation concrete actions and opportunities to get involved in serving children and families in poverty.

Each ministry and program I've mentioned can be performed by any number of individuals and relies on a diverse array of age groups, experience levels, time commitments, and passions to make the programs happen. Also, many of the programs can be done at little or no cost to the church's bottom line. Another important aspect of these ministries is that they can be scaled up or down depending on the size of your volunteer pool or the resources you have available. In other words, you can size your commitment based on what you have, and it will be win-win for your church and the school, the students, the staff, and the community.

5

PRACTICAL TOOLS AND TIPS FOR YOUR PARTNERSHIP

5

PRACTICAL TOOLS AND TIPS FOR YOUR PARTNERSHIP

From what I have shared in previous chapters, you as a leader or part of a church should feel empowered with ideas and principles when seeking to build partnerships between schools and churches. Once you've identified a partner and begin moving forward, there is always a chance you'll make missteps and mistakes. When a partnership is being developed, you should consider some practical tips and tools as you seek to implement programs and ministries. These tips can prevent a number of early mistakes.

Through this chapter, these helpful ideas are meant to provide a simple, direct way to be a better partner from the beginning of the relationship.

Follow Up and Build Relationships

For this section, let's say you've established a working relationship with a local school, you've identified needs that the church can uniquely meet, and you just started a new ministry with the school. From the time the partnership begins, the church leader for the partnership, be it clergy or laity, should maintain consistent contact with the school administration or with the person charged with maintaining the partnership from the school's end.

When I first started working at Floris, I managed the partnership with Hutchison the way I managed many partnerships with local organizations: on an as-needed basis. In a missions and outreach role for a church with multiple partners, I found it challenging to keep track of partnerships, leaders, and volunteers. Many of my relationships with social service agencies are transactional. While maintaining the connection with the school worked quite well, it did not help us build a better relationship with the school or with the administration. Our relationship was missing the intentionality that occurs when you build relationships. It's this intentionality that transforms partnerships.

Through my connections in the community with other clergy and faith institutions with school partnerships, I was able to learn a lot about other churches and their relationships with schools. I found out one church administrator met the principal at their local school partner on a monthly basis. Meeting regularly was a part of their partnership. To say I was jealous was an understatement!

Often we can look at our partnerships with other organizations as strictly tactical and transactional: we communicate only when one party needs something or has a question. But the work of the church should be relational first, tactical and transactional second. Around the time I learned of my colleague's monthly meetings, Hutchison Elementary received a new principal. From our very first meeting, I indicated a strong interest in building a relationship with him and his staff. I wanted to meet with him on a monthly basis, even if agenda items were sparse or nonexistent. He agreed it would make sense to do this.

I can't express how important this is. If you want to know a school better, you have to understand, even in the small ways, how the administration and staff envision their work and how they strive to improve the education and lives of the students. You must also know what vision the administration has for the future of the school. Oftentimes, and I am guilty of this in our ministry, we look at our relationship only through the lens of our ministries. But you must seek ways to understand the school better, and this can happen through regularly scheduled meetings. Over the past year, I can safely say I've learned more about the school than I did over the previous five years. And it was my own fault for not asking for the time to meet regularly.

If I can give any encouragement here, it's this: go to the school and sit down with staff on a regular basis, even if it's just to see how things are going. Remember, as Christians, we are all ministers and are seen as such by the community. Our partnership should not just be about what we get out of it or what our congregation provides. When you get to know the school better, you can find yourself celebrating with the school on its successes, mourning in its challenges and losses, and working with it to secure better futures for children in the community.

Goals and Outcomes

One of the harder things churches struggle with related to community service and partnerships is our ability to measure goals and outcomes. I'll even go a step further and say it's very rare to see churches set goals and outcomes in these types of partnerships and programs. A lack of goal setting isn't inherently wrong, but without it, churches are unable to have honest conversations about whether the ministry made the intended impact. When goals are set and then discussed at the end of a preset length of time, ministry, volunteers, and school staff are able to determine if a program was successful. Some may believe because these types of ministries and programs are run by volunteers, they do not need the scrutiny of goals and outcomes. But I disagree. Often volunteers would benefit from parameters and clear expectations specifically because they are not paid to help. They do it only because they want to, and they want to do a good job.

When thinking of implementing a program or ministry, the question that must be asked is rather simple: what does success look like? The good news is there are two typical ways this can be determined.

NUMBERS

Specifically, you can look at the number of people involved or the number of children/people served through the ministry. For example, if you are starting a mentoring ministry at a school, you may say getting fifteen mentors would be considered successful the first year of the program. Another way to look at this would be looking at a weekend backpack meal program. Let's say that the school would like to serve one hundred children per week. Well, success would be serving those hundred students every week for the entire year.

OUTCOMES

Outcomes, in the simplest sense, are perceived changes through action. For example, for a mentoring program, you could look at two possible outcomes, with one looking at those who volunteer and those who are served. For volunteers, one of the outcomes would be that at the end of each year, a significant portion of your mentors choose to commit to another year. If your mentors are returning, that means they've had a great experience and want to commit more time and energy to the students. On the other hand, a way to measure the outcomes of the mentoring would be to look at the performance and behavior of the students being mentored. If students are more attentive, getting better grades, and attending school more often, some of these changes could be at least somewhat attributed to another positive adult interaction in the student's life.

Admittedly, measuring outcomes is never easy between two organizations, as their goals and objectives can be different if not discussed regularly. The important thing for congregations to consider is how they are going to measure the church's success as well as the school's.

Building Project Plans

Once you've decided to start a particular ministry in partnership with the school, building a project plan is a good step. The purpose of any project plan is to map out the tasks required to make a project happen, identify who would be responsible for each task, and, if applicable, attach a deadline to completing the tasks.

While any number of Google searches will provide you with hundreds of task management options, I encourage you to find what works for you. Some people use their phones, others still like to use paper. Because project plans for ministries tend not to be long and exhaustive, sometimes a blank sheet of paper or an Excel spreadsheet will do.

When project plans are built in Floris's ministries, we first ensure that all the parties involved know what they are responsible for and when they need to have the tasks completed. For example, prior to our ESL ministry beginning each year, we meet with our leaders to go over expectations and tasks. The good news is that many of our ministry leaders have been doing this for a number of years. Usually when we meet only slight adjustments are needed. Some of the tasks may include:

- Design and print flyers for distribution.
- Call and e-mail the past year's volunteers to see who is returning.

- Recruit new volunteers.
- Reserve the space for classes at the school.
- Order books and supplies.
- Plan and lead an orientation.
- Recruit volunteers for registration.
- Manage the day-to-day operations of the classes.

Project plans are put in place to keep leaders and volunteers accountable to one another, especially in volunteer-driven situations. When expectations are clear, people serve better because they know precisely what their responsibilities are.

Three Areas of Impact

Churches should take the time and consider the resources required to make a ministry happen. In the case of many people-driven ministries like mentoring, you won't need significant financial and material resources. But you probably want to consider the time and energy it will take to recruit, train, oversee, and thank your volunteers for their service. Everything, at the end of the day, has a cost of some sort.

One of the questions I am asked on a regular basis is how churches should decide which programs and ministries they offer to the community and the world. I wish there was a secret formula I could share. Part of what churches and schools need to do together is determine whether the resources required for the ministry are worth the outcomes or goals set and whether or not they are achievable. In order to make decisions about the ministries and programs your church or organization offers, you have to consider three areas of impact. They are:

1. The impact of the program on the people served. How many people will you help, what type of help are you providing, and will it change lives for the better?

2. The impact of the program on the people who serve. Is it tangible and meaningful work that will impact a person's discipleship and service?

3. The impact on financial and material resources of the church or organization. Is it financially possible to continue this ministry for a sustained period of time?

As churches grow, so do their programs and ministries. This growth isn't necessarily done strategically. It's not because of negligence. Rather, churches often spread themselves thin because of the numbers of interests members in a congregation have. Increasing ministries may be a good thing. But churches need to go deeper in ministry, not by doing more, but by doing more focused, transformational work in a strategic fashion. If given the options, I would choose five ministries with one partner than five ministries with five different partners. Note: It's important for new ministries to fit in the context of your congregation or at least in a direction the church may be going. Vision requires understanding what excites the church. A sense of what the church cares about matters a great deal.

What Volunteers Need for Success

TRAINING AND ORIENTATION

For any ministry requiring a significant commitment of time from your congregation members, you should consider what training and orientation may be needed for your volunteers to be successful in the ministries and programs where they decide to give their time. Conducting trainings and orientations for your members working at a school is of utmost importance.

For a mentoring orientation, a sample agenda may look like this:

- Welcome
- Prayer and devotional
- Introductions
- About the school
- How to be a mentor
- Child safety requirements
- Basic logistics
- Tour of school

An agenda for a summer program may look similar:

- Welcome
- Devotional and prayer
- Purpose and logistics of the camp
- Volunteer expectations
- Handling child behavior

- Child safety requirements
- Breakout groups and tour of school

CHILD SAFETY CERTIFICATION

Because congregation members will be working with children, you will want to follow your church's policies on child safety. This may include, as it does at Floris, a background check, acknowledgment and review of child safety policies, and child safety-related training. In the case of Floris, we follow our policies and the policies of the school system, which requires all volunteers to get fingerprinted and receive a badge through the county school system. While some may see this as double-checking their volunteers, I would suggest it's better to be safe, as independent entities rarely share data on background checks.

In our case, because we live near Washington, DC, Floris has many individuals working in law enforcement and the Department of Homeland Security. Even so, if they work with children on behalf of the congregation, they must follow the guidelines as set in our child safety policy. If your church does not have a child safety policy, I strongly encourage you to get one in place immediately for the protection of the students in the community, the children in your church, and those who seek to serve them. The United Methodist Church has many resources available for churches developing child safety policies.

INFORMATION AS A TOOL

What tools and information do your volunteers need to do their jobs well? This can be logistical information such as times, dates, and locations. It can also include information about when and where the volunteers should give their time. It can include a glimpse into how a ministry or program plays into the greater picture of the partnership. Additionally, when working at the school, you should discuss the potential challenges that can arise through the interactions the volunteers have on a daily basis. Volunteers should be made aware of any potential safety issues, emergency procedures, and a person to contact, including a phone number, if they run into difficulties.

Volunteers should also be provided with technical knowledge, or tools, on how to do their volunteer jobs. The greatest tools for your volunteers are training and information on how to do their job well and what to do if they run into challenging situations. For something like mentoring, volunteers should not only know when and where to meet their children, but they should also be given tips and ideas on what to work on or do while they are together. The volunteers should also be made aware of what to do if they learn something of a sensitive nature, such as abuse at home or children needing help with basic needs like food. Volunteers should get an understanding of the school as a whole and its staff.

Most of our orientations and trainings include a staff member who will tell the volunteers about the student body and about how the program supports the school's efforts to educate kids. By having school staff present, volunteers get a better sense of the school as a whole and why their work is important for the well-being of the students.

DEVOTIONAL

Church staff or laity should also lead a devotional during orientations and trainings. It's very important that volunteers understand how their time and energy are an extension of their faith and representative of the church, and thus, it should be given the utmost commitment. In other words, you want to set an expectation that they are the hands and feet of Christ in this work of partnerships.

Learn from Others

As you start a ministry or program within your partnership, I encourage you to do what you can to avoid duplicating efforts and starting from scratch. As you are able, seek out other churches and institutions dealing with the particular issue you are trying to confront. When you work with schools, you will certainly run into challenges uniquely pertaining to your school partner or the surrounding community, but you should do your best to not reinvent the wheel.

For example, one of the easiest ways for a church to partner with a school is through providing food to the kids or the surrounding community. It may be through a snack program, a weekend meal program, or some other iteration. Remember churches or institutions across the country are dealing with this issue in creative, sustainable, and impactful ways. More times than not, these institutions have resources to share and lessons they have learned over the course of their programming. Seeking out information in this fashion will help you be more successful as you seek to meet a need.

Also remember, many issues churches deal with are very rarely new ones, but rather new instances of age-old problems such as hunger, poverty, and other types of needs. Experts in these fields, social agencies, and churches in your community and/or in other places are meeting these needs. Instead of spending a significant amount of energy trying to figure it out on your own, ask around and learn from others.

A good example of this occurred in the past few years at Hutchison. We decided, in partnership with the school, we were going to fund after-school programs through a large financial campaign called Imagine. Having very little experience managing or implementing after-school programs from a church perspective, we sought out multiple organizations and churches in the surrounding communities with after-school programming experience. We took the time to schedule meetings with them to better understand how they work, what challenges they encountered, and what, if anything, they would change if they were starting over. Of course, this is in addition to getting to know the details and logistics of the programs such as cost, schedules, curriculum, and logistics. Using this information, we worked over an extended period of time to develop a proposal process for the school as it developed after-school programs. Meeting with other churches and organizations gave us the knowledge and background we needed in order to maintain accountability and mutual expectations with our school partner.

This work culminated with the church making a significant financial investment in students at the school. At the onset of the 2016–2017 school year, our congregation presented the principal with a check for forty-two thousand dollars as the first installment of support for after-school programs at the school. The funds will support highly focused programs for nearly two hundred students in the fall and experiential learning experiences, such as field trips, for students who can't afford them.

If I've learned anything in my years of nonprofit and faith-based work, churches spend an inordinate amount of time trying to build programs and ministries from scratch without considering or learning from the institutions, faith-based or otherwise, already meeting those needs. A significant amount of overlap in services to the community may happen because organizations and churches are more concerned about creating their own programs instead of working collaboratively with other organizations. Please save yourself time and energy by researching and talking to other nonprofits.

Be Open to Change: Evolution Happens

If something isn't working properly, adjust it or let it go. Sounds simple, right?

Ministry work is hard. Have I said that yet? Church-supported ministries have spiritual implications for those who serve. When people live out their spiritual lives through your programs and ministries, they become very attached to those they serve and how they serve them. This makes change especially hard. It is one of the primary reasons that many churches have ministries that are five, ten, and twenty years old that should've been let go years prior. When passion and spiritual lives are involved, letting things go can be really hard.

In a previous chapter, I mentioned the clothing sale we ended after years of ministry as an example of a program we let go because it no longer served the needs of the school. The school asked us to discontinue this ministry. This is an example of open and honest discussion leading to significant change or elimination of ministry. More than anything, you need to be prepared to let things go or adjust them so you are always seeking first to serve the school in the way that makes most sense for both parties. Even if you and your school partner are happy with the progress and impact of your ministries, you should still make changes and adjustments if that is going to help improve the overall impact. Here are two examples.

When Camp Hutchison began, we focused our energies on reading, math, and enrichment classes such as arts and crafts, drama, and science. As we sought to evolve and make the ministry better, the school and the volunteer leaders indicated a strong interest in incorporating character education into the ministry. For a church working in a school, one could say that helping children develop character traits such as generosity, service, and kindness makes a great deal of sense. As one of my interns, Mary, suggested, we had a sincere interest in teaching the children how to be kind, respectful members of society. And who better to do this than a church?

Over the next few years, we added a puppet show to the camp for the students to learn about different themes each week, such as friendship and teamwork. Children received notebooks with games, quotes, and coloring pages that reinforced the learning. The interns worked with the volunteers to ensure that the reading and math lessons also incorporated those themes. By incorporating character education, we were able to not only impact the children's education, but also how they interacted with people and society.

Another example of being open to change is our English as a Second Language ministry. It is interesting to note we made changes based not on our work with the school staff, but rather the feedback we received consistently from our adult students and volunteers. When I first came on board at Floris, the ESL ministry was managed by a small team of volunteers who managed two ten-week sessions each year. One was in the fall, the other in the spring. Each session consisted of a registration, ten weeks of classes, and a celebration dinner. Even though providing ESL classes this way worked for a number of years, there were still some challenges.

First, many of the committed students attended both the fall and spring sessions and thus were required to register and pay twice per year. Second, registration required significant volunteer resources and, despite the fact that we held two registration days, we would often register students up until four or five weeks into the ten-week session. Third, we were unable to consistently find volunteers to manage the snack break, and the leaders often had to manage that as well. The teachers and students also found that the snack break unnecessarily took them away from their limited learning time.

In 2015, we made several changes to improve the ministry. First, we changed the two ten-week sessions into a program that serves students from September to April. Second, we removed the snack time and added a half hour to the class time. With these simple but bold changes, we have found better participation from students and volunteers and less work for the leaders who manage the ministry.

The important thing to note is we were able to make consistent improvements through collaboration and through feedback from the school, volunteers, and the people we serve. While change can be hard, it's hard to argue when people work collaboratively to make things better. It isn't always easy, but sometimes it's absolutely necessary.

Talk about the Difficulties, But Don't Overdo It

Our church was in the midst of a capital campaign when I met with the principal about making a video to highlight the partnership we had with the school. The interview questions I provided her focused primarily on the issues the children faced in their home lives and education. As we discussed these questions, she asked me to consider how I represented the student body to the church. I don't remember her exact words, but they were along these lines: "Jake, when you talk about the school with your congregation, you tend to focus on all the challenges that the students and school face—and no doubt we have our challenges. But we are a school full of bright minds, diversity, and amazing staff. We have lots of challenges, but we are also a great place for growth and learning. Let's try to focus on giving a more balanced view of the school."

This suggestion was important for one primary reason. By talking only about the difficulties, I was potentially framing the school to be seen as a place to pity, not a place of excitement for partnership. Compassion fatigue, a recently coined term, is a real thing. In essence, I could be dehumanizing the students and school staff with the congregation to a point of fatigue rather than motivating members to action. Wearing people out is the opposite of what we are trying to do! It's important for your congregation to understand the challenges, but don't talk about it to the point where it almost feels hopeless. Schools, even ones with significant challenges, have areas they celebrate and unique characteristics making them special places of learning. Try to give a balanced view.

Be Good to Your People

A word to the wise: if your clergy and laity leadership has done a good job of presenting the partnership and subsequent ministries, many people will get involved. Many of these individuals will see their volunteer time as an integral part of their spiritual lives. The human resources of a church and how they are deployed in the community are much more important than we tend to believe. It's not quite like a programmable rotisserie oven, where you set it and forget it. Rather, good ministries require good people, and you should check on them regularly to ensure the success of your ministry.

This is especially important for ministry leaders. On an annual basis, and sometimes even more often, I meet with ministry leaders to find out how they are feeling about their leadership and the ministry as a whole. We instituted these conversations because, if at all possible, we wanted to minimize and even eliminate volunteer burnout and fatigue. When ministries first start, ministry leaders may take on a leadership role without any consideration for how long they are interested or willing to lead.

Just as many administrative church committees have term limits, conducting conversations about whether a leader wants to continue in a particular role is a good practice. Having these conversations shows that you are interested in the health of a ministry and its leader. Typically, we aren't interested in replacing people who are still passionate, but we have these conversations to let leaders make graceful exits if they choose. When you do this, your leaders may still have the energy to give to other ministries in the future rather than completely back out of ministry leadership because they are burned-out and exhausted.

If your church is managing ministries led by volunteers, I encourage you to consider having succession conversations. The beauty of these discussions is each time you have one, the ministry leader is either making a commitment for another year, which he or she consciously and prayerfully must consider, or the leader is helping you find his or her potential replacement. One of these conversations might feature questions like these:

- How are you doing?
- How do you feel the ministry is doing? Are there any changes you envision in the future?
- How do you feel about continuing in this leadership role?
- If you're not continuing, do you have someone in mind to take your place?

Few things are more deflating than seeing a highly engaged, passionate ministry leader burning out because he or she worked on a ministry too long, didn't get the help he or she needed, or didn't feel as if the church supported his or her ministry. If you have any sincere interest in doing ministry well, you must take care of your people. Talk to them regularly. Ask them how they are doing. See where there may be opportunities to support and help.

Building a strong partnership can take significant time and energy to do well. As with most relationships, there are times where you will do great work and times when you'll have to regroup and rethink programs you've developed. That's the nature of this work. With these tips and tools in mind, building and maintaining lasting partnerships is within your congregation's reach.

6

HOW TO ENGAGE YOUR CONGREGATION

6

HOW TO ENGAGE YOUR CONGREGATION

As you seek to engage your congregation in the work of a school partnership, communication will be of utmost importance. In this chapter I will present ideas and strategies for church leaders and clergy to engage their congregations. As well I will identify the different ways leaders of the church, be it clergy, staff, or lay leaders, can engage and inspire action from the congregation on issues such as church/school partnerships and children living in poverty.

The Importance of Worship and Relationships

The primary way we can inspire our congregations to action is through weekly worship. Worship is the busiest time of the week for churches and it's when you have the largest possible audience for sharing the news, ministries, and events of the church. If you are seeking to enhance and build partnerships, you should definitely consider worship an opportunity to build your coalition of interested members. Whether it is sharing an announcement before worship, incorporating information into the actual worship service, or hosting a partnership-related event after the service, Sundays offer you the best opportunity to gain traction within your congregation.

While Sunday worship is the vehicle by which you can reach the most new volunteers and those willing to give time and resources to the partnership, another primary way we can engage volunteers in the work of a partnership is through one-on-one conversations and leaders working with members of the congregation relationally. In other words, the leaders must get to know people and be comfortable with having lots of individual conversations. The size of the congregation does not matter; there is no substitute for meeting face-to-face and asking people, in person, to be a part of a ministry.

Believe in Abundance

You are most likely a clergy or church staff member, or an engaged layperson who wants to consider partnerships with schools as a means to engage your church in local missions. Working with schools and children in poverty also may be a personal crusade for you. Maybe your life was impacted in a unique way by loving people, and you want to pay it forward. Maybe God is stirring your heart for children in your community living in poverty. You've spent time researching opportunities, meeting with school administrators, teachers, and potential leaders, and even considering the resources required to make a partnership happen in the near future. The possibility of partnership is starting to feel real.

You have been amazed at the response you've received from the school and from your friends at church. The church leadership seems interested as well—in fact, you see your pastor as a champion for a partnership with the school. You've worked with the school to determine the first of what you hope are many opportunities to impact the students and the staff. You are on the verge of communicating your first ministry opportunity, and you want to get the church really excited about this new endeavor.

But as you look at all the different ministries and programs occurring in the church, and the long list of worship components that the pastor has to accomplish each Sunday, you start to think announcing this project or partnership may not be the best thing. You are also concerned about the vitality of your congregation. Are they really going to get excited about helping kids? You are worried about overwhelming people, so you want to let people know about this partnership only through one-on-one conversations, which is important but only part of the bigger picture. Generally, you are feeling anxious about the success of your partnership.

While this is a scenario I hope doesn't happen in your ministry setting, God knows we get so caught up with doing more and more, we often do not give the important things enough time in front of the congregation. Our current culture is one of information overload, with different media craving our attention every second of every day. It's easy to think people won't be interested in this new ministry or it's just going to be one more thing in a laundry list. Thinking that no one is going to care about this work that you believe will be transformational is very easy.

First and foremost, get this belief out of your head. You've spent weeks and months getting to better know your community and the needs are there. You've learned the stories of children, families, and school staff, and you believe your church has the resources necessary to make great things happen. This background work has impacted you in profound ways. The important thing now is communicating the story to the church. You've prayed over it again and again. God has put these children and this school on your heart.

When you are designing new ministries and you bring these to your congregation, please remember this simple concept: When you are doing just and good work, work that honors God, work that helps those at the margins, you must believe fully and totally God will bless it and you will be successful. And you have to remember your mindset should be one of persistent abundance and optimism. If the God of the universe, our creator and redeemer, blesses our work, who is to stop good and just things from happening? When you believe this work will bless people and you and your church will be blessed in turn, this attitude has an amazing impact on volunteers, especially if you can connect the work to people's faith.

If you are going to be a champion for this ministry, you have to be able to share why it's important for your congregation to help. Your attitude has to be one of confident entrepreneurship. Here is what it should look like:

- You must believe the work you are going to do will make a difference.
- You must believe when we act justly, generously, and kindly, we honor God.
- You must believe God delights in our serving those who are oppressed and at the margins.
- You must believe God will bless the work you do, even when it seems hard, even when it seems out of reach, and even when you really struggle.

Scripture is filled with moments of doubt and concern, but also of hope and redemption. It is filled with freedom from the ills of this world and a beautiful vision of God's kingdom. Building great partnerships is not always easy, and getting people to commit to a ministry or a new partnership doesn't happen overnight. Creating and maintaining a partnership can create challenges and conflict, too. The work of the church in the community isn't easy. But if you believe God is sending you in this direction, you have to believe there will be a way to get things done. The church has lasted for a long time because people, empowered by the Holy Spirit, made the decision to give their lives to others in some capacity. In your congregations, power, resources, and impact are waiting to be harnessed. With new programs and ministries, you must put out the right message and pray that the Holy Spirit will get your congregation moving.

Build a Compelling Message

In order for a church to focus its mission and outreach efforts on children in poverty, church staff and key leaders must make a compelling message and cast and maintain a vision for what the congregation should do. Without providing your congregation with the theological and practical foundations of working with children at local schools, you cannot expect a significant response. You can engage your congregation in a number of ways.

First, church staff and key leaders must make efforts to connect the spiritual life of the congregation to community action and engagement; our actions and our involvement in community efforts of justice, mercy, and compassion affect our sanctification in Christ. Service to the community is a means of discipleship. As shown earlier in this book, partnering with local schools aligns with our traditions and our theology and can be transformative for those who choose to commit to service. With more and more people in need of an understanding and practical application of compassion and social justice, we must put people to the work of Jesus in this broken world. School partnerships bring about wholeness and positivity to children and to the community.

As the church we must be engaged in the community if we want to be relevant to our culture. This engagement is necessary if we are going to make disciples of Christ for the transformation of the world, as the United Methodist church proclaims as its mission. Any church hoping to bring people closer to Jesus must translate into the wider culture. Christ was emphatic that serving the poor was serving him. The call to serve the oppressed is not an optional request, rather, an integral duty to God and to our neighbor.

Making sure people know their work in the community is part of the Methodist tradition is very important. As I've mentioned, one of the glowing lights for Methodism is our roots in community work, our denominational history of serving the community, and of loving our neighbor. Methodist tradition includes the founding of schools, hospitals, feeding programs, and even newer initiatives such as Imagine No Malaria. By partnering with local schools and investing time, energy, and resources in children, you are continuing this legacy of compassion matched with action.

Second, we must make efforts to cast a vision for serving children living in poverty. Share this vision through church communications such as your website, social media, and print media, and through the worship experience. Sunday drives success for missions and outreach, especially at the outset. For a church/school partnership to be successful, it is very important for conversations to occur during worship regarding children in poverty, poverty in general, justice, and the partnership the church has with a local school.

Finally, you may also want to empower your congregation by sharing the goals and vision of a partnership with a local school. Help people understand why this school should be a mission zone, along with any pertinent information discovered through your time of learning and relationship building. Whether you are sharing about the partnership as a whole or a particular ministry or program, explaining the why is imperative, especially when you ask your congregation to give their time or their resources.

AN EXAMPLE

What might this look like? Earlier in the book, I mentioned a nearby elementary school in a more affluent neighborhood that had opportunities for mentoring students with special needs. Let's pretend a congregation has indicated an interest in partnering with the school to provide these mentors. How would you approach this with the congregation?

Primary is sharing the vision via worship or other communication mechanisms. An announcement from a pastor may look something like this:

> As many of you are aware, leaders of the church have been meeting with the local elementary school. Through these conversations, I have learned many of you have children attending this school. By getting to know the principal, the staff, and getting to know more about the families with children at this school, we've discovered a very unique opportunity for the church to stand in the gap and be of service to the children and staff.
>
> Our church has always been a generous one, not just in your service to the community and within the church, but also through your resources. In my time here, I have found you always welcome new opportunities when we discern the Holy Spirit moving us in a particular direction. One of the ways the Spirit has moved me, and many of our leaders, over the past few months is to serve children in need in our community.
>
> I believe our church truly cares about children. You see it in our ministries here on Sundays and

through the work we do locally and internationally. We are invested in kids' futures. This love for the wholeness of children is also etched in our Christian identity. God's preference has always been and always will be for the most vulnerable: the children, the person with disabilities, the orphan, and the widow.

As the staff and I learned more and more about the school and dug deeper into the opportunities and challenges it faces, we found out the school has one of the largest programs for children with disabilities in the county.

There are inherent challenges in educating children with special needs, especially since the school's budgets have been so slim the past few years. The principal has asked us to consider providing mentors and helpers for these students. These mentors and helpers would build positive relationships with the students, assist the teachers with a myriad of duties, and serve in other ways as needed. The principal believes that having help in these classrooms would make a remarkable difference in how the school can provide support to these children.

I am asking you today to prayerfully consider becoming one of these mentors. The leadership of the church feels so strongly about this opportunity that we have made a commitment to the school to provide a minimum of fifteen mentors ready to start in the fall. Mentors will make a weekly commitment to the children, they will have to undergo training on how to work with children with special needs, and they will have to complete child safety requirements. I know this is a big ask, but I want you to know I have committed to being a volunteer this year. With something this new to us, I also want to experience firsthand the work of our church at the school. A few members of the church council and another group of leaders have committed as well, but we still want to hit our goal of fifteen mentors.

I am not looking for answers today, but rather, will you pray about this opportunity? Is God calling you to be a part of these children's lives? Is the Holy Spirit moving you to respond to this request from our community? After the service, I will be in the gathering area with one of our leaders to answer questions and receive contact information for those who are interested in more information or are ready to get involved. Serving children with special needs in our community is a worthy endeavor, it is God-honoring work, and I hope and pray that you'll join me.

A bulletin announcement may look something like this:

> Come to the gathering area to learn about a new opportunity to serve children in our community. Sign up to become a mentor for children with special needs at the local elementary school! A weekly commitment will be required and training will be provided. For additional information, contact the church office.

You may want to develop a short description that leaders are able to share very easily with others, like an "elevator speech." An elevator speech for your leaders as they seek new volunteers may look like this:

> We believe that God is calling us to better serve our community, so we are developing a partnership with the local elementary school to begin a mentoring program for children with special needs. If you are able to make a weekly commitment and have a sincere interest in serving children with special needs, we will train members of the church so that we can have the greatest impact on these children.

Recruitment Ideas and Principles

It may sound redundant, but the partnership must be brought to the congregation's attention on Sundays. This may be through a strategically placed sermon series on community engagement or you can hold special missions Sundays or recruitments. The important thing to remember is you must make every effort to put the partnership on the forefront of the church's mission. You can do this during sermons, prayer time, inviting school administration to speak during worship, and announcements prior to worship. In this section I will provide some simple, actionable ideas you can use in your ministry setting.

One of the things that I am always cognizant of is the challenge volunteer recruitment and management can be on a church staff or on laity. While people may think that volunteer recruitment is rather easy, doing it well can be challenging if you don't have the right tools in your toolbox. With that in mind, here are some tools and ideas you should consider as you are recruiting for your ministries.

MINISTRY IS ALWAYS RELATIONAL

This may be the tenth time I've mentioned the power of relationships. It is key. Whether you need fifty people or five, building relationships and talking to people one-on-one will always make you more successful as you seek volunteers. While having the pastor do a pulpit announcement is very effective to inspire the congregation, making sure you have a table or a place for people to gather who are interested in more information will create opportunities for discussions and questions to be answered in a timely fashion.

BE AS CLEAR AS POSSIBLE

This applies to discussing requirements, time commitments, and any other pertinent expectations or logistics. You should share all information that helps people make a decision about committing time, energy, and resources to a particular ministry. You must be aware the requirements and expectations of a ministry may be too much for some people. While that fact may be deflating, it is okay. Do not, and I repeat, do not make your requirements and expectations lax just so more people will be involved. When you are creating your expectations, you should be thinking about the people you are serving, not those who are serving.

I've mentioned that for our mentoring program, volunteers have to be fingerprinted and given a badge through the county, in addition to completing our orientation and safety requirements. All in all, it can take three to four hours to get everything done. If I have an interested volunteer who really isn't willing to complete these requirements, how can I expect him or her to commit to meeting with a student each week for forty-five minutes to an hour for an entire school year? It's best to let your expectations and requirements do the thinning of the crowd for you.

KNOW WHY PEOPLE SERVE

Understanding motivations is very helpful in crafting your messages to individuals and groups. Using the example of a mentoring program for kids with disabilities, what are some of the reasons people would volunteer? Here are just a few.

- They have a dear friend who has a child with a disability, and they know the joys and struggles of that situation. They want to be a part of a community that supports children and families in these situations.

- They are passionate about education, and this is the first time they've seen an opportunity to work with kids that really makes sense.
- They feel needed. The pastor and laypeople have made a compelling argument, and they have not been too involved over the past few years. This is the right opportunity at the right time.
- They have retired and need to do something that matters with their time.

When you understand why people get involved in a ministry or program, you'll better shape the recruitment language. In looking at the reasons I've just listed, you could easily highlight particular items when you're talking to people or giving talks about the ministry. A good practice generally, for all your ministries, is to find out what drives a person to participate.

RECRUIT APPROPRIATELY

The way you recruit should also match the commitment required. For example, if you were going to do a packaging event for a backpack meal program and there is no sign-up required for the one-hour event, a recruitment message may sound like this:

> Hey friends, we are going to put together some backpack meals this weekend for the school. No sign-up required, just come and serve. Packaging the meals should take an hour, so bring your family and let's get this done!

Now, imagine using similar language for a mentoring program for children with disabilities:

> Hey friends, we are going to start a mentoring program at the local school. It will require weekly commitment for the school year, and you'll need four hours of specialized training and other safety orientation. We hope you'll join us next week for the training!

As you can see, using the same language for ministries that require different levels of commitment isn't necessarily the best idea. It's best to be up front and clear about the commitment level required. To give you more insight about some different opportunities, let me provide you a few more examples of ways you can recruit for ministries.

- For our mentoring program, we invited the principal to speak at our morning services, not just to ask for more mentors, but also to thank the congregation for being great partners for so many years. Having a staff person from the school is really key. It's one thing to request service from a pastor or a layperson; it's another thing entirely to have the principal make a plea for partnering. This alone will yield more responses, especially from folks on the fence about helping.

- You could show a short video about the kids and their mentors. Over the course of the school year, take time to interview some kids, with the school's permission, about their experiences with a mentor. The video doesn't have to be perfect or filled with bells and whistles as long as it's from the heart. I am by no means a great video editor, but I can create a thirty-second promo video that will help people choose to be mentors. What a great opportunity to engage others in your congregation who have video editing and videography skills: put them to work. And get folks to tell their stories!

- Have a table outside the sanctuary where people can sign up and ask questions. Be there with the principal and your mentor leader. By having three people, you can have many conversations in a short amount of time.

- Place a bulletin announcement for at least three weeks and have the pastor give a pulpit announcement encouraging people to sign up.

- Offer follow-up that week for those who sign up. Ask volunteers to provide their preferences as to which days and times work for them, whether they have a gender preference, and whether or not they'd be willing to mentor more than one student at a time. Provide them with the requirements and orientation dates.

Here are a few other simple things you can do:

- Host a school partnership meal at the church where people can come to learn about the school and the ministries you hope to start there.
- Have clergy or another leader visit small groups and Sunday school classes to encourage folks to sign up to help.
- Create a Missions Sunday Fair that showcases all the mission opportunities at the church.
- Try to create high-volume, low-commitment opportunities to do something for the school, such as packaging meals for kids or doing a school gardening project or grounds cleanup— anything to get more members involved.

With these ideas, I am certain churches seeking to build partnerships can make an impact by doing high-quality volunteer recruitment so that your ministries are successful.

INSPIRE ACTION

We must convey the needs of the children at the school while also offering concrete means for the congregation to respond. This is of utmost importance because it can be very disheartening to people in your pews when they learn about all the hard things children face without tangible ways to respond. At Floris, we provide facts and anecdotes about children in need and children in our community to the congregation when necessary, along with our hopes of serving children in poverty as an integral part of who we are as a church. When we have these conversations, we also try to be strategic in offering different opportunities for the church to be involved in serving the school and the community.

Our opportunities are diverse regarding the type of work and commitment involved, the time of the year the opportunities occur, and the amount of commitment involved. Talking about poverty and offering ways of fighting poverty must be done in conjunction whenever possible. Essentially, you are striking when the iron is hot. For the Floris and Hutchison partnership to be successful, conversations about the needs in the school and our biblical and denominational call to serve the community were regular parts of our communications and were almost always paired with an opportunity to serve the school in some form or fashion. In 2017 and beyond, we are doing much more strategic work to invite the school staff and administrators to the church on a regular basis so the congregation can put a face to the partnership.

MAKE THE PARTNERSHIP
PART OF THE CHURCH'S IDENTITY

Ultimately, the partnership must become an important aspect of who your congregation is. It must be ingrained in the culture if you want it to succeed. Otherwise it will be just one more ministry for a select few of your members. Floris has striven to be known as a church that cares about children living in poverty in our community and abroad. As mentioned previously, Floris and Hutchison have a collaborative relationship that spans more than fifteen years. In that time, the church and school have worked together on multiple programs and projects to serve the students and staff of the school. Many members of the congregation are able to articulate a description of our partnership and how it impacts the school and their own personal faith journeys. This is precisely because when we made efforts to communicate a vision of serving children in poverty, we made compelling arguments to our congregation to inspire action, and members of the church made the decision to have the partnership as a part of their spiritual lives.

GO FOR DEPTH,
NOT BREADTH, IN MINISTRY

I mentioned earlier in the book that I have a deep appreciation for churches and organizations that give focus to their work. So, for example, if I had to choose between four ministries with one partner or four ministries with multiple partners, I would choose the former. The reason is because that focus on a particular organization, or a particular issue, if spoken about enough in your congregation, will infiltrate the culture and DNA of the church.

I like to tell people that no matter how many ministries you are doing, the people you are recruiting, inspiring, and educating in your congregation are giving you a certain amount of attention and airtime. So let's think about it like a delicious apple pie. If I have to split it between four people, they each get a pretty big piece of pie. But if I have to split it between twelve people, the slices are much smaller. When you have twelve people who want pie, the pie does not magically get bigger. Thinking of this analogy when you communicate missions and ministries to the church, whether you have ten ministries to share or three, the attention given is about the same.

There are many things in our world vying for our attention. If depth in ministry is important, you must consider focusing your efforts in such a way where ministries align with a particular partner or with a particular mission area. That way, when you are talking about it, people are not just giving you their attention at that time, but rather they are reminded of this focus, this area of care, and the interest their church has in a particular issue.

Working in specific partnerships or in specific areas of focus allows your church an opportunity to dig deeper and be a part of something bigger. A sense of unity and impact can make your church members see and believe in the power of collective work. If your church decides to focus on a particular issue and a handful of people want to go in another direction, I strongly encourage you to let them investigate and spend their time and resources in the way they choose. I am a firm believer the church can't be all things to all people as an institution, but we certainly can encourage people to follow their hearts and passions around the things they care about. But it's also important to say just because a member cares about something doesn't mean the church should have to do something on the same issue.

TALK ABOUT THE PARTNERSHIP REGULARLY, BUT NOT ALL THE TIME

Just a quick final note about engaging your congregation. Please talk about the partnership regularly and offer opportunities for your congregation to respond, but don't talk about it all the time. I mentioned compassion fatigue in the previous chapter; it is a real and present thing in the world of missions, outreach, and volunteer management. The partnership should be important and well-known, but don't beat people over the head with it every single Sunday. Spread it out, give people a break. If you ask people to volunteer for things every Sunday, people will eventually start getting numb to the opportunities. The good news is that many opportunities related to schools are seasonal. So you'll probably talk about it just when you're doing recruitment and maybe when you're ending the program for the year.

Communicating a new ministry or partnership well can help ensure success for the long term. Providing compelling messages, aligning the congregation's DNA to the task of school partnerships, and using simple, yet effective recruitment ideas will allow you to bring your congregation to the task of serving children in your community. And remember, you've done the work to get you to this point and God has blessed this work thus far. Believe in the abundance of God's love and mercy and see where this partnership takes you!

7

SEEING THE IMPACT OF A PARTNERSHIP

7

SEEING THE IMPACT
OF A PARTNERSHIP

In this final chapter, I will talk about how to understand your church's impact and how ultimately this work with schools plays into the discipleship of your congregation. Finally I will share some context as to where I believe this movement toward church and school partnerships is going in the future. We are on the verge of a movement, led by so many congregations with existing partnerships, toward more congregations joining with local schools across the country to seek wholeness for vulnerable children.

Seek Mutuality

Before we began our work with Hutchison, many conversations with church members, school staff, and other key people occurred to ensure we viewed partnerships between schools and church from different angles and perspectives. Over the course of the past year, one of the people I've spent a lot of time with is Ray, the principal at Hutchison.

Through these conversations, one of the things Ray said was rather simple: when any group has an interest in partnering with the school, he wants to have a sense of their goals and outcomes to make sure they are aligned. At the same time, he wants the partner to know what his goals and outcomes are. This way, when discussions of partnership come up, the school and the partner have mutual understanding.

Because Floris and Hutchison had an established relationship with many impactful programs and ministries, our conversations about goals and outcomes have been ongoing. We are constantly updating and improving ministries. When Ray started at Hutchison, it was important that I shared how Floris envisioned the partnership, but it was also important that Ray had space while he was learning about the school. Remember, his primary responsibility as a new principal wasn't to satisfy the wishes of partners but rather to inspire learning and lead the school toward excellence.

More than anything, I wanted him to know how much we cared for the school. Beyond seeking to meet the needs of the students and staff and seeking wholeness for vulnerable children, we see the partnership as a means of discipleship for the congregation. We don't partner with schools just because it feels nice to do good things. We are called to love God and love our neighbor. Hutchison Elementary School is our neighbor. If we believe our work in the community is a means of growth and transformation, we must be servants in the community.

There is much to love about our partnership and our goals for the partnership, but what makes our partnership powerful is that the school is a place where members of our church can engage their community, build relationships, serve, and grow in their love of God and love of neighbor. The school, in a sense, is an avenue of spiritual growth for our congregation. Our partnership is a spiritual relationship.

The aspirations for this partnership go deeper than the discipleship of individual members of the church. When a partnership digs deeper and creates significant impact, it becomes interwoven into the culture of the congregation, so much so that the congregation and the school are seen as a single community. This idea of a unified community may sound optimistic or cheesy, but we are resurrection people who hope and pray for God's kingdom.

When you commit to a partnership requiring the human resources of your congregation, you must understand this work as a means of grace for those who serve, but beyond this service is real and true transformation. Relationships are a means of justice and community renewal. Once you get to know people who struggle in their day-to-day lives, once you acknowledge that the child in the Title I school is beloved by God, your heart starts to open and the Holy Spirit will do things beyond your imagination.

Any ministry can be skin-deep. When you are building a weekend meal program or a summer camp, it's very easy to look at the work as a good and just thing. Your church members can feel proud about the work they do to fight hunger and provide kids with excellent opportunities. The questions are much different when a church begins to ask why so many kids in your community are hungry and why your county schools aren't doing more for children with little or no resources. As you build a partnership with a school, you have to understand this idea. For a real relationship, for real community, for deep transformation, there is no telling how deep you can really go with a school once you see each other as one community.

One of the stories brought to my attention during the writing of this book was of a young boy I'll call Luke. Three different people talked about him and what the church did for him and his family. Luke was a promising student, but he experienced a number of challenges. The primary challenges were his family had very little income and limited English proficiency. His teacher and one of the Floris volunteers who acted as a classroom assistant began noticing he was growing noticeably sicker. He struggled to stay focused, and his body was swelling. After they talked to his mother, she took him to a doctor and he was given some medications, but that didn't seem to help.

After another day of not feeling well and experiencing swelling he was sent to the nurse's office and our volunteer went with him. The Spanish speaking counselor and our volunteer discovered he had gone only to the emergency room and hadn't actually been seen by a pediatrician. His mother didn't have a primary care physician because of a lack of resources. Our volunteer was able to connect the family to a pediatrician in the church. Through medical testing, they discovered the boy had a form of leukemia.

Our volunteer, Pat, reflected on this experience with Luke and saw "how much Luke suffered with every step he took on our way to the school nurse that day, and how he cried. His mother had been putting larger and larger shoes and clothing on him in an effort to comfort him on the outside. The language barrier made it very hard for his mother to grasp any part of his medical crisis, and I could see it in her eyes that she 'knew' her son was going to die; just as one of his cousins died from some form of stomach cancer the previous year."

From this point on, the church mobilized to get Luke into the right children's medical program at no cost to the family. Luke's mother was a single parent and had limited transportation and other children to take care of, so church members stood in the gap by providing rides for Luke to treatment. Church members helped the family financially with things such as groceries, and the church supported Luke and the family in countless other ways. Because of this partnership, a young boy and his family were able to connect to resources that helped him go into remission. The church rallied around Luke and his family, and it was a unifying moment for the partnership. If I know anything, I know this: the church, when it stands in the gap for vulnerable children and shows boundless compassion to families in need, we are doing the Lord's work. Our partnership allowed us the opportunity to minister to a family that was suffering the effects of disease. Luke's story represents what's best about a partnership between a school and a church. If one of our hopes in working with schools is that we build relationships and better community, standing in the gaps for a child and his family fits that mold to a T.

Signs of Transformation

As you build upon your partnership and more and more of your congregation begins to volunteer and engage in the ministries happening with the school, you should expect to hear stories of transformation. Any time people are willing to give, assume the experience will have a transformative effect. You shouldn't expect the world to upend itself because so many people are giving energy and effort to children and staff. But you should expect that gradual transformation will occur in some fashion.

In those leading the ministries and programs, look for a few signs of a great, transformational experience. Some signs of transformational experiences are returning volunteers, their willingness to share about their experiences, their ability to recruit friends to participate, and their ability to talk about the importance of the program. As a means to publicize and bring attention to these ministries, you should consider asking people about their experiences on a regular basis and share what you've learned. Build relationships with your volunteers. There will be stories to tell, and it is incumbent upon you and other leaders to tell the story.

When I was doing disaster recovery work in New Orleans after Hurricane Katrina, a trainer came to speak to our staff one day. He suggested every team participating in disaster relief should spend time getting to know the homeowners they were helping. If the team and homeowners met, the team would learn their stories. From there, the team would tell their friends and neighbors when they returned home. This continual storytelling would produce future teams and engaged individuals. Our ability to tell our own stories and getting others to tell their stories is a great way to keep the partnership in front of people and inspire action in those who are not yet involved.

VOLUNTEERS WHO STAY WITH THE PROGRAM

One of the telltale signs people are being transformed and impacted by a ministry or program is that they come back. For those programs that are volunteer-intensive and require a significant commitment, returning volunteers usually means they have decided the particular ministry is an integral part of their lives. This may not always be the case, as sometimes ministries and programs are just really fun and people enjoy them. Joy and fun are important, too.

As an example, our mentoring program usually has a 70 percent return rate, give or take a few percentage points. If thirty mentors were at Hutchison this past year, we can confidently assume at least twenty are going to come back. The mentors who do not return usually fall within a few categories. First, the mentor may have had a significant life change at home or at work, conflicting with the mentoring schedule. Second, the student the mentor was working with may have gone to another school. Finally, some mentors won't really enjoy the experience—they discovered it wasn't really their forte. While some may consider this deflating or a failure of some sort, I think it is a good thing when people better clarify their interests through participating in multiple ministries. This usually means they are actively seeking deeper discipleship and community.

In our mentoring program, we ask only for a one-year commitment. Very often we find volunteers will stay with the students for a number of years because they've decided the children they mentor are important enough to be a part of their lives on a weekly basis. Multiyear commitments are sure signs of transformation.

WORD OF MOUTH

Another sign people are being transformed through their participation in a partnership is they tell their friends. Using mentoring as the example again, you'd be amazed how many new mentors we get each year because a friend encouraged them to get involved. People who invite their friends to get engaged in a ministry almost always succeed in their recruitment. Friend-to-friend recommendations only heighten the status of a ministry amongst the congregation.

As mentioned previously, one-to-one recruitment should always be a part of a strategy, and having your volunteers tell their friends only enhances that ability. Your best recruiters are the volunteers who love what they do.

VOLUNTEERS WHO CAN SHARE RESULTS

Finally, you can see transformation when your mentors can articulate what the ministry means to them and their faith. When our mentors had an end-of-year breakfast with their students,

I was able to talk with a number of mentors. While they all talked about their experience differently, they were all able to articulate how important the kids were to them and how much they truly enjoyed being a part of a bigger partnership seeking to improve the lives of children.

Evaluating Your Work

If you've taken any time to read the latest mission-related books, you've probably considered how you are measuring the success of ministries. This is very important work. As I mentioned in previous chapters, all ministries should consider the three areas of impact:

- Those who are served.
- Those who serve.
- The resources required.

Consider these three items after a ministry to see if they produced and required what you expected. As necessary, you should make adjustments. The question you should always ask when doing ministries and programs is this: what are we trying to accomplish by offering this ministry?

Having an understanding of why you do something is smart. Try your best to keep it simple. When gathering information about a ministry, you have to look at the different ways one would evaluate success. One way would be the number of people you served, as I mentioned, and the amount of resources it took to get to that number. But also, how did those who were served view the resources provided to them? How did those who served, your volunteers, experience the ministry or program? Did they feel useful? Did they know what they were doing? One action step you may consider is doing surveys, informally or formally, with key participants after a ministry is completed. I try to keep mine rather simple, so I usually ask the following questions:

- What went well?
- What didn't go so well?
- What would you do differently?
- Are you willing to commit to this ministry again?

For some of the ministries, you may find it hard to get the data you need to know if you've really made a difference, especially if it involves asking the school. I have found asking the school for data in an already overbusy environment doesn't always work well, especially considering much of our work is a supplement to the primary instructional work the teachers and staff are doing.

The first year we offered Camp Hutchison, we were able to do pre-camp and post-camp tests, all of which showed we made a tangible difference. As the school looked at the data on learning over the school year, the summer program did not make a significant dent beyond leading students to keep learning over the summer months. Summer learning is well and good; still, we really hoped we'd have a more tangible impact. But if you think about it, three to four weeks with two hours of instruction per day over the summer is a drop in the bucket compared to the rest of the school year. Looking only at the educational component of Camp Hutchison takes away from the intrinsic value of much of our summer program. The children were learning, the children were in a safe place, the students had wonderful experiences they would cherish, and they had food to eat. From that perspective, you can only come to the conclusion you've made a difference.

Ministry evaluation is hard because you can't always measure the impact outside of the numbers. For mentoring, as an example, how can you really gauge success of a forty-five-minute-per-week program?

Herein lies the challenge. Keep to your goals, evaluate your ministries, and be accountable to the numbers, but also play the long game. In other words, think about the work you do in God's time, not your own. If we are genuinely seeking to improve the lives of vulnerable children, we can meet their basic needs, we can encourage them, and we can offer resources and opportunities. But we also have to believe God's will for all children is one of love, learning, and happiness. This may not always happen, but take comfort in doing all you can when you can.

If I can give you an example of long-game thinking, let me tell you about my prayers for some of the students at Hutchison. A few years ago, we made some pretty significant changes to Camp Hutchison. There was great excitement about one of the changes: we adopted an outer-space theme. Most, if not all, of the projects and learning we did during the camp reflected this theme. The kids read books and wrote stories about the planets and the solar system. The kids watched as our volunteers launched rockets. The kids created and painted space suits and space helmets. On the last day of camp, we even had someone from NASA speak to the kids about space. The awe and learning we saw in our campers was very inspiring for many of our volunteers and for the school staff. The camp was just plain old fun!

After the camp ended, I was able to share with many people about the outer-space theme and all the fun the students and volunteers had. I jokingly mentioned to people that we would know if we made a difference in the lives of these students if twenty or thirty years from now, one of them became a rocket scientist or an astronaut. It started out as a joke, but today it is my prayer. The prayer is not just for future rocket scientists and astronauts, which would be amazing, but for children to be inspired to reach their fullest potential. My fervent prayer is for children's physical, mental, and spiritual needs to be met today so they can fully live into who God has made them to be. This is the long game.

Understanding Your Impact

As I look back on the relationship we have with Hutchison, there are probably thousands upon thousands of moments that made a difference in the lives of students, volunteers, or the community as a whole. These moments are etched in the hearts and minds of those who experienced them. The impact of a partnership will come in waves. Sometimes the impact will be huge, noticeable, and swift. Other times it will be small and to our eyes, insignificant. If I can offer any encouragement to you in your journey toward a fruitful partnership, it is this: embrace the partnership, work together, and watch what God will do through you, your congregation, through the school, and through the students.

There are undoubtedly children in your community who could benefit from additional resources such as food, clothing, and shelter. Children in your community need mentoring and positive daily interactions with adults and other types of life-enriching resources. There are people in your congregation who are on the cusp of jumping into their faith, just waiting for the right opportunity. The Holy Spirit will spur these members on to live out their faith through works. As church or lay leaders, you get to live in the middle of this world where the needs of your community and the resources to meet those needs meet. It is here you will begin to understand the impact the church can have and the power a congregation has to be a change-maker in the community.

As missionaries to the community, you are going to see the worst of situations people endure and the best of people's hearts. Living in the middle of hope and darkness is one of the hallmarks of the church. To me, this is gospel living. More than anything else, I want you to understand not just the way you live between these two realms, but also to understand the power and the majesty in you, in your congregation, and in the community you serve. When you understand this, the impact becomes much simpler to recognize, as it all connects to the kingdom work you're doing.

Discipleship and Relationships

As I reflect on the hundreds of volunteers who have given their time to the school in some fashion, I am constantly reminded of the ways our members are impacted by the time they give. People usually begin to volunteer out of an intrinsic need to be helpful and make a difference. You hear this sentiment often in the volunteer world. In faith communities, many people are driven by their faith. But what I have found to be true is that those serving often feel the benefits in such a way they no longer see themselves as giving but rather as receiving the benefits of service. I am sure you've heard something like this: "You know, when I started, I wanted to volunteer because I knew the kids could really use the help. But these kids have helped me more than I ever helped them."

There is a certain beauty to service, of giving oneself to others, that helps us grow as people. And as those who are driven by our faith to work in the community, we'll find a certain growth in discipleship will always occur when we give of ourselves sacrificially and commit to a cause. We discover our deepest spiritual nature when we serve others in the name of Jesus. In Methodism, we believe that discipleship is a constant, forward-moving sanctification that makes us more and more Christlike. This movement toward loving God and neighbor more fully is abundantly clear to those giving themselves to children in need.

I am a firm believer, and this has been confirmed more and more through my work, that the greatest means of personal transformation and discipleship happens when a person commits to building meaningful, loving, and mutually beneficial relationships with other people, especially those at the margins of society. In the case of the school partnership, this may mean mentoring a child, befriending a teacher or administrator, or helping an immigrant learn English. It is in this shared friendship and community where true discipleship happens.

When we encounter situations where we not only get to know other people but also through relationship building become brothers and sisters, life-changing discipleship happens. When the members of your congregation see their faith life lived out with those living on the margins, you will begin to see the fruit of this work. From the United Methodist Church's website, we see how the institution of the mainline church views service to our neighbors and communities, as it describes mission and service through our Wesleyan Heritage: "Because of what God has done for us, we offer our lives back to God through a life of service. As disciples, we become active participants in God's activity in the world through mission and service. Love of God is always linked to love of neighbor and to a passionate commitment to seeking justice and renewal in the world."[29]

Join a Movement

To conclude this book, I want to share a few reflections as you and your congregation consider building or deepening a partnership with a local school.

First, what drives my interest in church and school partnerships is imagining a future where children and the fullness of their lives is encouraged, facilitated, and offered through God's church. If more churches considered making schools and vulnerable children in their community a priority, what would be different? What changes would occur in the students served by the church? What changes would occur in those who serve? How would your community be different if groups came together to put energy and investment in education?

Second, if you're on the fence about starting a partnership, just do it. If you choose to do nothing about the problems and challenges in your community, such as making sure the children in your community have the resources to thrive, if you never take a stand on particular issues like hungry kids, and if you never fill the gap for vulnerable people by ensuring children have adequate supervision in the summer, you can't expect the world to be different or transformed or for the problems to solve themselves. Jesus set an uncompromising path of compassion, love, and grace, and we have to be bold enough to follow. Get your hands dirty with the problems of your community and see where God brings you.

Starting a new partnership with a school involves taking risks and showing up. In my opinion, taking risks and showing up are hallmarks of successful ministries to the community. We don't have to be perfect, we don't have to have all the problems figured out, but we do have to try. Children in our community deserve our attempting to make the world better. Making the decision to embark on new ministries is never easy, but frankly, difficulties and challenges are present in all great endeavors. If it were easy to correct problems, the world would've been fixed years ago. Churches do their best work when they're willing to put resources into an endeavor. Hear this loud and clear: any resources you put into children, even if the endeavor appears to be a failure, will always be worth it. If your church can say it's made a difference and it's willing to take a risk to improve the lives of children in its community, then you've made the right choice.

Also, keep it simple. Success doesn't require complexity. By building good relationships, by seeking to understand the context of your community, success will come one way or another. With the practical tips and ministry ideas provided throughout this book, making a difference is not far away.

Finally, and on a personal note, I am thankful for this opportunity to share about the partnership between Floris and Hutchison. The work involved has not always been easy, but it's been worth all the energy, time, and effort. This partnership has changed my life, and I know it has changed the lives of children and members of the congregation. This partnership has been a blessing to see unfold, and I am eager to see where the partnership goes in the future. There is inspiration for partnerships everywhere. Hundreds of churches are offering awesome, life-changing ministries in partnerships with schools. One such program that I heard about recently is Project Transformation. This organization utilizes college age students serving children in urban communities. Abingdon Press, the publisher for this book, has developed an amazing character education curriculum for churches to use in schools called Love in a Big World. These are just two instances of great things happening for churches and schools. Wouldn't it be amazing if thousands of churches and schools partnered together to make a tangible impact?

It is my fervent hope and prayer that we join in a collaborative environment where every school wanting a church partner has one, and thousands, no millions, of children's lives are improved. This prayer may be ambitious, but I like to think God appreciates this type of ambition and God will delight in all movement toward this just work. As you seek to build meaningful partnerships within your community, remember the tools and tips in this book. While no book on this subject can fully articulate the opportunities and challenges inherent in building great partnerships, this is a great place to start. I encourage you, beyond anything else, to put yourself and your church in a situation where you can delve deeper into the community, as it is then I believe your church will find its passion.

NOTES

1. Tavis Smiley and Cornel West, *The Rich and the Rest of Us* (New York: Smiley Books, 2012), 64.
2. Smiley and West, *Rich*, 68.
3. Smiley and West, *Rich*, 118.
4. Smiley and West, *Rich*, 53.
5. http://schoolprofiles.fcps.edu/schlprfl/f?p=108:13:::NO::P0 _CURRENT_SCHOOL_ID,P0_EDSL:287,0. Accessed December 10,2016.
6. National Low Income Housing Coalition, "Out of Reach 2015: Low Wages & High Rents Lock Renters Out," May 19, 2015, 227-229. Statistics from http://nlihc.org/sites /default/files/oor/OOR_2015_FULL.pdf and calculations from http://nlihc.org/library/wagecalc. Accessed December 15, 2016.

7. http://schoolprofiles.fcps.edu/schlprfl/f?p=108:18:::NO::P0
    _CURRENT_SCHOOL_ID,P0_EDSL:287,0. Accessed
    December 10,2016.

8. Eric Jensen, *Teaching with Poverty in Mind* (Alexandria:
    ASCD, 2009) online free chapter.

9. James Cone, *God of the Oppressed* (New York: Orbis Books,
    1975), 8.

10. Smiley and West, *Rich*, 112.

11. Pamela Couture, *Child Poverty: Love, Justice, and Social
    Responsibility* (St. Louis: Chalice Press, 2007), 24.

12. Couture, *Poverty*, 33.

13. Ibid.

14. Albert Outler and Richard Heitzenrater, *John Wesley's
    Sermons, An Anthology* (Nashville: Abingdon Press, 1991),
    179 "The Marks of the New Birth."

15. Shaun Causey from devotionals for *Camp Hutchison
    Manual* (May 2011), np.

16. Jürgen Moltmann, *Jesus Christ for Today's World*
    (Minneapolis: Fortress Press), 19.

17. Moltmann, *Christ*, 28.

18. Outler and Heitzenrater, *Sermons*, 555.

19. Abhijit Banerjee and Esther Duflo, *Poor Economics*,
    (New York: PublicAffairs, 2011), 39.

20. Smiley and West, *Rich*, 53.

21. Malcolm Gladwell, *Outliers* (New York: Little, Brown, and
    Company, 2008), 258.

22. Annie E. Casey Foundation, "Early Warning! Why Reading
    by the End of the Third Grade Matters" (Jan. 1, 2010), www
    .aecf.org/resources/early-warning-why-reading-by-the-end
    -of-third-grade-matters/. Accessed December 20, 2016.

23. Gladwell, *Outliers*, 256–259.

24. Susie Swan, Virginia Turner, and Jake McGlothin,
    Camp Hutchison Manual (May 2011), 1.
25. Ibid.
26. Ibid.
27. Ibid., 2.
28. Ibid., 2.
29. http://www.umc.org/what-we-believe/our-wesleyan
    -heritage, accessed December 21, 2016.

ACKNOWLEDGMENTS

This book was created with the help of many people and institutions. The members and staff of Floris United Methodist Church are such an important part of my life. It is my pleasure to be a part of a worshiping community seeking to be at the center of its community. The people from Floris that I would like to thank include: Tom Berlin, Tim Ward, Linda Haselhorst, Susie Swan, Virginia Turner, Pat Terry, Shaun Casey, Susanne Jones, and Mary Frances Roll.

Much of this book was developed through my graduate work at Wesley Theological Seminary. The professors at Wesley taught me important theological lessons but they also helped me think about how to put those theological understandings into action—especially as it relates to churches engaging their communities.

I'd like to thank Ray Lonnett at Hutchison Elementary, Becca Messman, and Tim Warner, who graciously gave me time.

I am also thankful for the staff at Abingdon Press who made writing a book an absolute pleasure. I pray I wasn't too much of a pain!

Finally, I must acknowledge my mother, Gail McGlothin, who made the first suggestions and edits on this book. Her help was invaluable!